Praise for

The Referable Client Experience

The Referable Client Experience isn't theory or surface-level advice. It's a practical, clear-eyed look at how to build trust, create connection, and make it easy for your clients to refer you—without begging, bribing, or those awkward asks.

If you've ever wondered why your happy clients aren't sending more business your way, this book has your answer. *The Referable Client Experience* will show you how to generate referrals: with class, with clarity, and with consistency.

LUANN NIGARA, speaker, author, host of *A Well-Designed Business®*

In her new book, *The Referable Client Experience*, Stacey Brown Randall shows how to create experiences your clients can't help but talk about and how to turn those conversations into new business. From referral seeds to hot zones, Stacey provides a framework for sparking, nurturing, and growing referrals that come from existing and alumni clients.

JOEY COLEMAN, international keynote speaker and *Wall Street Journal* bestselling author of *Never Lose a Customer Again*

Want more referrals? Are you referable? Read this book, follow Stacey's system, and become a referral master. Stacey will show you how.

LARRY KENDALL, author of *Ninja Selling*

Stacey turns the art of client relationships into a science, with powerful results. This is more than a book; it's a practical roadmap for business owners who want referrals to become second nature. If you're ready to transform your client experience into your biggest growth engine, this book is your game changer.

JENNIFER GILLMAN, president of Gillman Strategic Group

What a powerful paradigm shift Stacey delivers for any business able to offer a truly tailored client experience. Instead of focusing on asking clients to refer, she shows you how to create a referable client experience. One approach is forced and awkward, the other is natural and practically unstoppable. Before you invest in any more marketing or sales funnels, implement Stacey's approach first. When you do, every dollar you spend on other ways of acquiring new clients will go twice as far.

SIMON BOWEN, founder of The Models Method® and creator of The Genius Model®

Stacey Brown Randall delivers a clear, practical roadmap that helps business owners turn great work into lasting relationships and reliable referrals. She shows us how to design a client experience that builds trust, strengthens connection, and earns referrals naturally, without ever having to ask. This is a must-read for those who want more business without chasing it.

MARK R. LEPAGE, AIA, founder of EntreArchitect

A refreshingly practical and human approach to building client relationships that drive growth. Stacey shows that referrals don't come from gimmicky tactics, they come from trust, connection, and doing the work that makes people proud to talk about you. This book nails it.

MATTHEW BARNETT, CEO and papa bear at Bonjoro

THE
Referable
CLIENT
EXPERIENCE

A Proven Method to Generate Referrals Without Asking

THE
Referable
CLIENT
EXPERIENCE

STACEY BROWN RANDALL

Cataloguing in publication information is
available from Library and Archives Canada.

ISBN 978-1-77458-593-1 (paperback)
ISBN 978-1-77458-594-8 (ebook)

Page Two
pagetwo.com

Page Two™ is a trademark owned by Page Two Strategies Inc.,
and is used under license by authorized licensees

Cover and interior design by Jennifer Lum

referableclientexperience.com

To those brave enough to jump into business ownership,

you make the world a better place.

Let your light shine bright.

To my mother, Mary Ella Brown.
Thank you for my competitive spirit and for serving
as a constant reminder that you can be a wife
and a mom—and bring home the bacon.

Contents

Introduction

A S I CHECKED OUT of my hotel in London, I asked the concierge how to get to Heathrow Airport. He called a cab for me, which I didn't think much about. When the cab arrived, I loaded my luggage, settled into the back seat, and watched the passing scenery while I thought back over my epic trip. As I relived my two-and-a-half week backpacking excursion around Europe, missing my flight was the last thing on my mind.

The ride dragged on. I checked the time—panic rushed in. I asked the driver how much longer, and his answer was not what I was expecting. By his calculations, I would arrive at the airport about the time my flight was boarding. Then he said, "You know, the fastest way to get to the airport is by the tube, not a cab." It was a little too late for that piece of brilliant information.

I ended up missing my flight and had to stay the night at the airport hotel because the next flight back to the States was the following morning. How had I gotten into this situation? It had started with not asking the right question. I hadn't asked the hotel for the fastest way to get to the airport, nor had I shared what time I needed to be there. I had just asked for a ride to the airport.

In this case, the risk of asking the wrong question was minimal; I made it home just fine, if a little late, and only for the cost of a one-night hotel stay. But my missing flight correlates to the risks many small business owners take when they ask the wrong questions or spend too much time asking the good questions, but at the wrong time. Questions like "How can we make bringing on a new client more efficient?" or "How can we put a process in place to lessen or eliminate clients needing to reach out?" aren't bad. But when business owners ask these questions at the wrong time, or in the wrong order, they risk missing opportunities to improve the client experience.

For twelve years, I have worked with small businesses in the professional services and creative industries. I see the same struggles over and over again. There's a tension between running the business more efficiently and making the business more referable and successful. The result? With a continued focus on speed, efficiency, ease, and finding the easy button, small businesses inadvertently eliminate (or downgrade) one of their strongest competitive advantages—connection with their clients.

Without that connection, getting referrals from your clients is, at best, an uphill battle. Creating a repeatable, referable client experience—one that produces referrals from your clients without asking those clients to refer you—is nearly impossible. You need to nurture that connection. To do that, start asking different questions of your client experience, questions that help you add connection into the equation and that build relationships with your clients, making you referable in the process.

What specific questions should you ask? Let's start close to home: If I asked you what it is like to work with you, as a client, how would you answer? To go a little further: If I hired you and your company, would I refer you to other potential new clients? Would I refer other business owners, my best friend, or my mom to work with you?

Do you know what it's like to work with you from your client's perspective? What is the value—to your client—of doing business with you? Not value as in the dollar number you'd put on your business to sell it, but value in terms of offering clients the services that they need, along with an experience that fosters connection, relationship, and referrals to new clients. What I'm talking about here is offering the value of an intentional client experience. Not just in the work you do for clients, but in the way you foster connection with them.

Maybe you feel like you have heard this message before. I thought I had; sometimes it feels like I've read everything ever written about the client experience. You too? The thing is, while there have been some great books and articles written about the client experience, there has also been a lot of noise. And something is missing from most of these publications— information about how to create the specific type of client experience that generates referrals.

So, I urge you to cut out the noise and ignore the shiny objects, the could-dos, and the wouldn't-that-be-cool ideas that often surface when you talk about client experience. Instead, get clear about exactly how to deliver the best client experience possible—the one most effective in generating referrals—and how that can help you grow your business.

Before beginning, it might be helpful to look a little closer at what the client experience actually is so you can read this book with your client experience lens clearly focused. To sharpen that focus, let's step into a business that is perhaps a little different than the ones you and I run—the restaurant business.

Growing up, I spent a lot of time with my grandmother. She owned many restaurants, known in the South as fish camps. A fish camp is a restaurant that serves mostly fried seafood on metal army trays like the ones you may have seen in the television show *M*A*S*H*. These restaurants offer sit-down dining, and the food is excellent. Not exactly healthy, but delicious and addictive.

My grandmother's fish camps were all in South Carolina. Her best one, the Lake Bowen Fish Camp, was situated, per its name, on a lake. My mom helped part-time with managing the books and then eventually progressed to running the floor on the weekends (she worked at the fish camp in addition to her full-time sales job). When I was younger, my brother Jeff and I would tag along and do odd jobs. In time, we had real jobs there every weekend. You name it, I've done it: host, cashier, waitress, busboy, dishwasher, takeout. I just wasn't allowed to cook (a badge of honor I still hold today).

From my perch at the hostess stand, I watched my mom direct the floor—her control of how employees greeted and sat customers at their tables was a thing of beauty. Every Friday and Saturday, the line of a hundred–plus hungry customers snaked out the door and curved around the building. And every Friday and Saturday, more people joined the line. Do you know what makes people still stop to eat at your restaurant even when they see a line out the door on a busy night? Knowing that they won't stand in that line for very long. My mother orchestrated their movement every night so well that they knew they would be seated in record time. After just one dinner, customers realized they would have an excellent experience at this restaurant, so they kept coming back and told their friends.

The restaurant customer experience holds many lessons for evolving your business's client experience. If you are an attorney, business consultant, interior designer, CPA, architect, real estate agent, business coach, or financial advisor—that is, a small business owner who becomes the trusted expert for your clients—you need to do what my mother did so well: carefully orchestrate your clients' movements through the complete client experience.

Granted, a restaurant's customer experience happens much more quickly and repeatedly than other experiences. It is generally completed, from start to finish, in the matter of an hour, with hundreds of customers on a rotating basis. This volume and speed make the client experience easier to establish and repeat. But the principles are the same in any services-based firm. While your client experience lasts longer per client, it means you must pay greater attention from start to finish, as any dropped balls and communication gaps can have greater consequences over the long run.

Plus, the stakes are arguably higher. Your average client isn't spending fifty to seventy dollars when they hire you. Typically, they are paying thousands of dollars to work with you. That's what makes your ability to provide a repeatable process that delivers excellent value and nurtures the relationship paramount to your business.

I wrote this book to help you do just that. This book will give you space to think about your client experience, whether you have an intentional experience that needs improvement or an unintentional experience that happens by default and needs a complete rework. To leverage what you learn for your business, you'll need to use this space to think and to assess; I

Your ability to provide a repeatable process that delivers excellent value and nurtures the relationship is paramount to your business.

encourage you to engage with the exercises included in these pages or complete them in the companion workbook. They are built to help you become crystal clear about what your client experience could be. When it's time to pause and do an exercise, you should stop and do it.

Your motivation for fully participating in each step along the way? By the end of this book, you'll have the foundation in place to implement a repeatable client experience that wows your clients and generates referrals. But it's important to remember that building your referable client experience means playing the long game. It's like building a domino train: You have to put one domino piece in place at a time. Placing each one takes you one step forward until all the pieces are in place and ready to go. That's when you can unleash the energy.

If you read my first book, *Generating Business Referrals Without Asking*, you already know how amazing it can be to receive consistent, sustainable referrals that you don't have to ask for. But you know those referrals won't just drop into your lap without you first being referable.

This book will provide a roadmap to guide you and help you establish an easy-to-implement, cost-effective, and repeatable client experience that impresses your clients and generates referrals. You know that your clients won't refer you if they have a choppy or inconsistent experience. Not to worry, though; implementing a referable client experience is easier than you may think. You just need to shift your focus to consider the context of what your clients go through when they choose to do business with you.

Your client experience is a journey for your clients. Building your intentional, referable client experience will be a journey for you.

Let's get started, shall we?

Note: If you are using the companion workbook, each exercise I provide is included with step-by-step instructions. Using the workbook gives you one place to keep everything together.

Throughout the book, I will reference additional resources and examples that will support you. Since they can't all fit in the book, you can find those resources on our reader-only resource page at referableclientexperience.com/insider-resources.

PART 1

FEELINGS DRIVE THE EXPERIENCE

1

What Is It Like to Work with You?

"I DO GREAT WORK, Stacey. My clients love me and tell me how much they enjoy working with me. So why don't they refer new potential clients to me?"

The angst is real. So is the frustration. I've heard this same statement many, many times from small business owners. In my twelve years of teaching referrals, each time I hear it is as heartbreaking as the time before. In fact, it happens so frequently that I sometimes begin my presentations to groups and companies by addressing the issue. I start with two simple questions. You can follow along as well—don't worry about those staring at you as you seem to randomly stand up and down; you're doing it for your business. For the first question, I want you to stand up if the answer is yes. Ready?

First question: Do you do great work? Meaning, do you believe you provide a valuable offering to your clients that helps them attain the success they are looking for or receive the transformation or result they desire? (If the answer is yes, stand up.)

When I ask this question during my presentations, without hesitation, the entire audience usually stands up. I'm guessing you did too (figuratively or literally). Now, remain standing. For the second question, if you answer yes, you'll remain standing. If you answer no, you'll sit down. Ready?

Second question: Are you drowning in referrals? Are you receiving so many referrals every month or over the course of a year that you just can't keep up?

Thud.

That's the sound of everyone—typically every single member of the audience—taking their seat. Usually, no one is left standing.

Why?

Because, as counterintuitive as it may seem, doing great work and being valuable to your clients simply does not equate to receiving referrals. It's a hard truth to hear and accept. Logically, it makes sense that if a client loved working with you, they would tell other people and refer those people to you. If only that were how it works. While that is not the case, you can implement a way that does work. There are strategies and tactics you can add to your client experience to make you referable and help your clients start to actually refer you. The best part? These tactics and strategies do not involve asking or paying your clients to refer you.

The first step is to understand that to be referable, you'll need to focus on more than just the work you do and deliver for your clients. Don't get me wrong—doing great work for your clients is incredibly important. But the quality of your work does not make up the totality of the client experience. Nor is it sufficient, as many business owners believe, to address the client experience by only creating a customer service process or team to deal with issues or questions that arise.

Thinking that either approach is the totality of your client experience is wrong.

The client experience isn't the work you deliver or the troubleshooting support you provide. Client experience is how the client feels when they are working with you. So, yes, the work you do matters, but it's not the whole story or the entire equation. In the next chapter, I will dig into all the nitty-gritty details of the client experience, but first, I want to establish why the client experience matters, why it matters now more than ever, and what it is and is not.

Why Client Experience Matters Now

The client experience has always been a part of doing business. We just didn't call it that or understand it as well as we do today. As client expectations evolved, they took on a new form: Clients developed a heightened sense of needing more from the companies they chose to do business with. Essentially, the buyer (or client) grew; they abandoned the concept of caveat emptor (buyer beware) and developed expectations for how companies should treat them, anticipate their needs, and meet their expectations even without knowing they had those expectations.

For a long time, a company could succeed by leveraging price, improving performance by streamlining processes, and working to offer new and enhanced products and services. This meant the client experience was "relegated to post-purchase engagement and viewed as a cost of doing business." Then the Internet changed how consumers shared their thoughts about businesses. Online reviews and social media posts proliferated with comments and mentions that changed the landscape of how customers viewed and talked about companies.

Think about restaurant reviews. In the past, restaurant critics employed by a newspaper or publication conducted reviews, versus today, when anyone can go online and leave a review on Yelp or Google. When a restaurant critic was critical of your restaurant, at least you knew they had journalistic training, experience, and standards to uphold. Now, everyone can be a critic with just the click of a button. Even my teenage daughter won't check out a restaurant that has less than a stellar rating, a rating that is compiled by other customers of the restaurant who sometimes don't give the whole story of their experience in the review. In this new dynamic, consumers can share their experience and judge businesses by how they *felt* when doing business with them, not just by price and product performance. The spotlight that now shines on the feelings of clients and prospective clients shifts perspective—those feelings matter now more than ever.

And those client feelings drive the action clients take. According to Customer Experience Matters, a business advisory firm, your loyal customers are five times more likely to purchase again and four times more likely to refer a friend. No wonder more companies have shifted their focus to improving their client experience—they could see that establishing genuine relationships with customers would translate to loyalty and spending, as well as drive sustainable results.

Recent analyses suggest this interest in customer experience only continues to grow. A 2025 Forrester study of customer experience leaders revealed that "40 percent plan to increase their overall cx [customer experience] investments... in the next 12 months." This is only continuing a trend of corporations focusing on improving the client experience for more than the past ten years. For example, back in 2020, a Gartner survey revealed that almost two-thirds of leaders responsible for the client experience were planning on budget increases that year, which was an increase compared with the 2017 survey, where 47 percent of CX leaders expected budgets to increase. Going even further back to 2014, a Gartner survey forecasted that within two years "89 percent of companies plan to compete primarily on the basis of the customer experience."

Small Business Superpower: Tailored Client Experience (CX)

While all this data is important for business owners to understand and act on as the marketplace shifts right before their eyes, the research often focuses on solutions for big companies. If you Google "client experience," you will find an overwhelming amount of information on omni-channel, artificial intelligence (AI), machine learning, data analysis, multimedia learning, and more. As interesting as that information is and as solid as that advice may be, the prerequisite for using it is that your company must be a certain size and have a particular amount of resources available. That's just not possible for most small business owners and solopreneurs.

Over the years, I have stumbled upon client experience models, frameworks, and explanations that might as well be in Latin when it comes to the application of the model or framework for a small business owner. You need your own model. Small business owners and solopreneurs need to apply the knowledge and the details of a client experience differently for it to work.

So, how do small business owners best apply this knowledge? By leveraging what they have that big businesses lack, their size. While it's true that much of what small businesses know about the client experience comes from the big companies and corporations that first identified, utilized, and deployed it, I believe—as a small business owner—you actually hold the *greatest* ability to leverage the client experience precisely *because* you are small.

After all, who better to construct a unique relationship built on trust than a small business? Who better to create an impossible-to-copy client experience than a small firm where the clients have faces and names and stories, where they have actual relationships with you and your employees? Your superpower is your size because it allows connections at a level bigger companies can only dream about. I'll dive deeper as I move forward into what it looks like to leverage the connection allowed by your size, but keep in mind that I'm not talking about volume or quantity of connection, but quality.

Client Experience = How Your Client Feels Working with You

So, if client experience is so important, what is it, anyway? The definitive meaning of client experience is hard to pin down— businesses have been tackling the question for a while now. For example, Forrester defines client experience as "how customers [clients] perceive their interactions with your company." Others, like HubSpot, define client experience as what happens before a client even becomes a client: "the impression your customers have of your entire brand throughout all aspects of the buyer's journey."

Your superpower is your size because it allows connections at a level bigger companies can only dream about.

The easiest and most accurate way I've found to explain client experience is this: *The client experience is how a client feels about your company while doing business with you.*

Simple enough, right? Of course, how you deliver on that feeling can be complex if you allow it. To simplify the client experience, we break it down based on a series of work and relationship-building connection points (I refer to these as "touchpoints"), which you will explore in detail in upcoming chapters.

Client Experience ≠ Customer Service

Even though there is a fairly straightforward definition of client experience, most people don't use it yet. When I ask business owners to describe their client experience, they don't usually talk about client feelings at all. More often than not, they frame their response around how the business handles customer service issues. But customer service is only a part of the client experience. How you fix a problem or answer a question for a client matters, of course, but those exchanges don't add up in the same way as an ongoing, intentional client experience that drives how a client feels when working with you from start to finish.

Why not? Well, let's look at the *Oxford Advanced Learner's Dictionary* definition of customer service: "the help and advice that a company gives people who buy or use its products or services." There you go: Customer service is directly related to the product or service itself, not necessarily the *experience* the client has.

Impossible to Copy

Focusing on, and customizing, your client experience offers you a valuable opportunity to stand out against the competition. More and more companies are realizing this: According to Dimension Data, 81 percent of companies recognize the client experience as a competitive differentiator. In other words, they believe that their ability to stand out against their competition is largely rooted in their client experience.

And they're right. By taking the time to create and implement an intentional client experience, businesses can create a unique client relationship that becomes difficult for a competitor to duplicate. Use this approach, and your client experience becomes one of a kind. Impossible to copy.

To become impossible to copy, focus on defining, creating, and implementing your own intentional client experience—one that is unique to your business. You don't need to get fancy or complicated or use the latest high-tech solutions, though you can; you might, for example, decide to include technology in your client experience to drive efficiency, but only as part of the client experience. The important thing is to focus on being heartfelt and impactful and create a process that works for you—an experience you can handle, can teach to your team (if you have one), and can execute on every time you bring on a new client. After all, you are the one who has to build and implement your client experience; thus, your goal is to build a client experience that makes you referable without overwhelming you.

It will take some effort. But it's risky not to do it, because without a repeatable client experience, there is a greater chance for error in how your clients interact with you. Ultimately, this impacts how they feel about you, which will in turn impact your brand, your reputation, and referrals.

Think about it from the client's perspective: For someone to refer you, they are putting their own reputation on the line. That means they won't refer a choppy, crappy, or even "meh" (average) client experience. So, your first step is to become referable—worthy of receiving referrals.

Moving forward, be open to shifting your thinking to the type of relationship you are building with your clients as they move through the process of working with you.

Digital Downloads: Find the additional resources mentioned in this chapter on our reader-only resource page at referableclientexperience.com/insider-resources.

2

Give Your Clients a Reason to Love Working with You

"I HAD A LOT OF HARD KNOCKS once I started in real estate twenty years ago," Brian Stevens, a realtor in Pittsburgh, shared with me.

"In the beginning, I was looking at every person like they were dollar signs. I used to joke, I couldn't sell a house if I bought one for you. I viewed every client like a transaction, and I tried to get through it as fast as possible because I needed to figure out how to get to the next transaction, the next client. My clients were—unfortunately—just a means to an end. In that rush, I wasn't listening to my clients, and I certainly wasn't connecting with them. I wasn't looking at my clients like they were a person, like a friend or family member I was helping. Then a mentor told me to start listening to what my clients wanted and were saying to me and make sure I provided that to them. When I started listening and built a client experience based on what I heard, work didn't feel like work or a hustle. I enjoyed it."

With that advice, Brian started listening to his clients in a new way and asking different questions. He started to look at the real estate transaction from the perspective of what the client goes through—the client stressors, the unknowns, the joys. From there, he started to fill in the gaps for them.

What was one huge gap he uncovered? Moving boxes. You'll know what I'm talking about if you've ever had to move. You don't think boxes are such a big deal until you're packing up an entire home and you deal with the do-I-have-enough-boxes headache. From experience, I do believe you can never have too many boxes.

So, how does Brian use the box headache—that every one of his clients will deal with—to be a part of creating his intentional client experience? He provides a moving box kit for every room in the house. The kit includes all the things you need to pack up a room, including boxes, packaging material, a tape gun, and markers. The moving box kit is part of his white glove concierge service that all his clients receive, regardless of the size of the house a client sells. That means that no matter his commission check size, every client receives a box kit for every room in their home. He has built it into his client experience and executes on the same process for everyone.

Brian makes a key point that "if—as a client—you're made to feel special and you're listened to, it doesn't matter what happens because you know you're being taken care of."

Being able to recognize what your clients are ultimately after—that's what the client experience is all about. Brian's moving box kit touchpoint meets his clients where they are by alleviating a pain point; it also impacts how his clients feel about him, which is the heart of the client experience.

To those of you stuck on the price of those box kits, let me just say it's a worthwhile investment. Brian uses key moments like this in his client experience to help him generate future clients from his very happy and grateful clients. Brian knows some real estate agents who spend $200,000 a year on lead generation like Zillow, but he just focuses on developing a client experience that moves his clients to rave about him and to refer to him.

It's easy to see clients as dollar signs, just as Brian once did. Unfortunately, it's a trap many business owners fall into without ever meaning to in the early years of creating and growing their business. Taking the time to understand the different facets of the client experience will help you start to visualize your current client experience and allow you to identify gaps so you can improve it. Even better, you can create a client experience so your clients will actually love the relationship they have with you and your business.

Creating that unique, positive client relationship—through the client experience—will always start with putting yourself in your client's shoes and meeting their needs in ways they don't expect. How do you do it? Let's start with getting the basics in place.

When the Client Experience Starts

Your starting point is easy to define as it is the same for all businesses. The client experience, or CX, starts at the moment the client says, "Yes, I want to work with you," which means the client experience begins once the buyer's journey ends.

You may have previously paired the buyer's journey within the client experience in your mind with an umbrella term such as the customer journey or client journey. A lot of people think of it that way, but to me, the phases are distinct. After all, the buyer's journey and the client experience exist in two separate time frames, and you need to build them on different frameworks. Let's break down the buyer's journey to show where it stops and where the CX begins.

The Buyer's Journey

First, you need to understand the three parts of the prospect funnel—awareness, buyer's journey, and close—and how they fit together. A prospective client moves from stage to stage in order, but the pace of their movement through each stage can vary by their particular needs and sales cycle.

PROSPECT FUNNEL

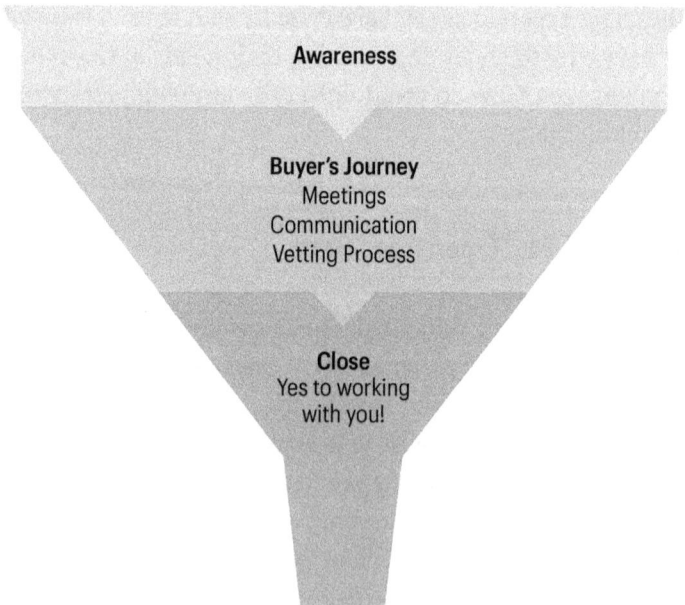

Awareness

Buyer's Journey
Meetings
Communication
Vetting Process

Close
Yes to working
with you!

The buyer's journey begins at the point when a prospect becomes a prospect *for your business.* They move from merely being aware of your business to actively pursuing a solution to a problem or need they have. The potential relationship you have with them is no longer theoretical; they now recognize they have a problem to fix or a need to meet, and they are interested in learning about the solutions you provide. With this buyer's mentality, they are taking the first step into your buyer's journey. Keep in mind, this doesn't mean that they aren't also buyers in a parallel buyer's journey with one of your competitors.

During the buyer's journey, the prospective client is trying to decide if they should hire you. They could be checking you out online, reading your reviews or testimonials, scheduling and attending a meeting with you, and reviewing your materials. They might have a couple of meetings with you while they're trying to decide whether you're the right person for them. If your buyer's journey doesn't include meeting face-to-face (virtual or in-person), you may chat with them on a phone call or maybe ask them to participate in one of your webinars.

The buyer's journey may be slow or quick depending on factors such as the pain level of the buyer (how urgent it is that they solve their problem), their budget, their capacity to get started, how quickly they move to the trust part of the sales continuum, and if they were referred or not. Sometimes the buyer's journey is super short. Think of a customer who needs a new winter coat and has heard amazing things about The North Face, so they stop by one of its stores or hop on its website and make a purchase. Or maybe a business owner is facing a problem that needed to be solved yesterday—that can speed up the decision-making process as well. Other times, the buyer's journey is much longer. For example, when a client decides to change their financial advisor or CPA, the process requires meeting with the potential advisors and taking the time to consider options.

Regardless of the length of the buyer's journey, buyers all go through this critical process of assessing the offer, considering how it might work for them, and deciding if they trust the person being hired to deliver—before they purchase anything. The decision to buy or hire, that is, the close phase, ends the buyer's journey with a yes, no, or not now.

When you hear yes, the client experience begins.

When the Client Experience Ends

The next valuable question is, When does the client experience end? If it begins at the same time for each business, does it end at the same time for each business?

No. The end date of your client experience is dictated by the type of work you do and how you deliver your service. For some, the work is never done, so the client experience extends indefinitely. Others can identify a firm date when the work will end. Still others, depending on the different services they provide, might be a hybrid of both.

A quick note before you dive into this section. My intent here is to help you understand the cycle of how you work with clients, but as I noted earlier, the client experience is not necessarily about the work itself, and it does not end once the work ends. As you will explore in later chapters, it's crucial to extend the client experience after the work is done, though you take different actions when a client is no longer actively working with you.

Work Types

To get started, let's look at an example of each type of work so you can determine which category your business falls into: ongoing work, firm end-date work, or a hybrid of both.

Ongoing Work

An example of ongoing work would be the work of a CPA. Every CPA's goal, with every client, is to prepare and file their taxes every year and to keep them as a client for as long as possible. It's all about getting ongoing work to continue every year.

End-Date Work

Interior designers, on the other hand, tend to do end-date work. Once the client approves the design and it is installed, the work is done. That doesn't mean this is necessarily short-term work; it might be an individual room in the house or a whole-home renovation or even a new build, all of which have different timelines. In each case, though, when it's done, it's done.

Hybrid Work

The third category is hybrid work. If you have projects that start and end but also have clients who are on retainer with you, your business is a hybrid.

A business attorney's office is one example of a hybrid business. Maybe some clients need the attorney for one deal, one negotiation, or one case. Other clients might have the attorney on a continuous retainer.

Determining Your Work Type

At this point, it's important you know when your client experience starts and when, or if, it ends. Decide now if your client experience is ongoing work, end-date work, or hybrid work. I'll walk you through the particulars in the upcoming chapters but, for now, determine if your business is one where:

A. Work has no end (ongoing work),
B. Work has a finish date (end-date work),
C. Work is both ongoing and has an end date (hybrid).

(If you are using the workbook, you can circle your answer there.)

The categories are fairly straightforward, but you may have some questions as you examine your work cycles. For example, if your clients end their work with you but come back later to do more work with you (repeat clients), that's also considered option B, end-date work. Those of you offering hybrid work will want to pay special attention to how the client experience starts to differ when a client is moving toward the end of the work with you versus when the client is staying on indefinitely. The goal is to make the variation minimal and easy to manage.

The Client Experience Journey

Now that you've identified the type of work your business does and, thus, when the client experience begins and ends, it's time to look more closely at what happens during the client experience journey itself. In this section, I will walk you through the three stages of the client experience and introduce the formula I use to describe what makes up the three stages.

The Three CX Stages

Client experience has three distinct stages: the new, active, and alumni client stages. How you work with your clients determines the client stages you will encounter. If you have ongoing work with clients, then your clients do not move to the alumni client stage but stay in the active client stage indefinitely.

The following is an image to help you visualize how the stages work together.

CLIENT EXPERIENCE STAGES BY WORK TYPE

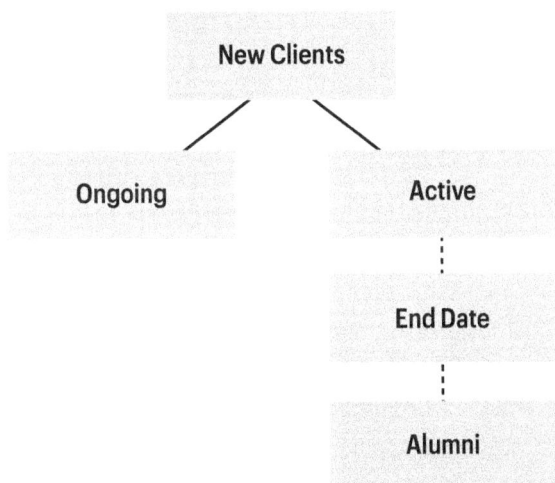

New Clients

Ongoing   Active

End Date

Alumni

Let's look at each stage in more detail.

New Client Stage

The new client stage is, as it sounds, the time when your client is new to you. It's easy to identify when this stage begins—the prospect has exited the buyer's journey by saying yes to working with you. It becomes a little more complicated to decide when the new client stage ends; that is dependent on the workflow within your business. For example, a business coach may decide that the new client stage ends after the first coaching session. Another example is a marketing consultant deciding that the new client stage ends after they finish collecting the data they need to provide their recommendations. Ultimately, you get to decide when your client experience moves from the new to the active client stage. As you move into part 2 of this book, I'll guide you through making this decision for each stage. For now, I just want you to have an understanding of each.

Active Client Stage

When your client exits the new client stage, they move into the active client stage. For some businesses, this is where clients stay. The active client stage for businesses with ongoing work becomes their clients' home for the foreseeable future. For example, for bookkeepers, the ongoing work repeats and continues every month as they reconcile their clients' books. For those businesses with end-date work, the active client stage also has a predictable end date. The active client stage lasts as long as it needs to for you to complete the work, project, or deal. For example, a real estate agent may determine that the active client stage ends at the closing table or when they hand over the house keys to the client.

Alumni Client Stage

Whenever the active client stage does come to an end, the client "graduates" to the alumni client stage. This doesn't mean the relationship is over, just that the work is done.

Why "alumni"? I know most people refer to clients who are no longer active as previous or past clients. But I want to shift your thinking on them. Think of them as alumni, just as a college thinks of its students after they graduate. Colleges cultivate these relationships—they want to stay connected to their alumni so they will contribute back to the school with support and donations. The kinds of donations you're seeking from your alumni clients are the possibility of them becoming repeat clients and, of course, sending you referrals. In this case, the alumni client stage has no end. In part 2, I'll break down how to handle the alumni client stage based on the volume of clients.

Now that you are clear on how you work with your clients and the three stages of the client experience, it's time to put everything together and explore how to use this information to deliver quality work and foster connection. To explain the formula for how these two fit together, I'm going to use an unusual analogy: the marriage proposal.

Tying the Knot: The CX Formula

How is the CX formula like a marriage proposal? Stick with me here. The client experience is made up of two parts—the work you do and the relationship you build—which are needed for it to work correctly and give you your desired result. And, interestingly enough, so is a marriage proposal (typically).

When you think about someone proposing, there are two parts to the proposal: the ring and the ask. The ring given is a physical symbol of the engagement; the ring is proof that a proposal happened. The ring, in a business setting, is the work itself, the service you delivered. It's the part that the client can touch and feel, so to speak, just like you can touch and feel an engagement ring. Like a newly engaged person, the client can show off the work; it's the part that others can see. It's what people will ask to see.

The other part of a proposal is less about what you show off—the ring—and more about how they were asked, how the proposal happened. That "how it happened" provides the story to tell. Was it on a hot air balloon ride, with family on Christmas morning, or on a quiet Saturday evening watching the sun set? How it happens then becomes the story the bride tells about the proposal. It defines and rounds out the proposal. The ask, in a business setting, is the relationship you are building with the client.

Using myself as an example, while I may show off my engagement ring because you can touch it and see it, what I talk about and share with others is how it happened, meaning the story of how Norm proposed. (If you're wondering, it was in a hot air balloon. He took the ring up a few thousand feet without it being insured, and it was a tad too big.)

Both parts make the proposal work: the engagement ring and the setting of how the question was popped. So, let me relate this to the client experience and specifically the two parts of your client experience formula.

The first part of the CX formula is the work you do—the physical evidence, a.k.a. the engagement ring, a.k.a. work touchpoints. The second part of the CX formula is the relationship you build with your clients, a.k.a. the story of the proposal, a.k.a. relationship touchpoints.

Here's a simple image to put this into context.

It takes both parts to make the client experience work.

CLIENT EXPERIENCE FORMULA

Great Work		Packaging
💍	+	🎈
Work Touchpoints		Relationship Touchpoints

Work Touchpoints

While work touchpoints are pretty self-explanatory, let's just spell it out for clarity's sake: Work touchpoints are the work you do for and deliver to your client. They don't need to be literal touchpoints. If you were my wealth manager or financial advisor, for example, I couldn't exactly touch that service, but I would probably receive regular statements showing what's happening to my money as you manage it. Other work touchpoints include contracts, paperwork, communication, and any other output or deliverables you provide for your clients, whether they can be touched or not.

Most businesses boil down their client experience to a series of work touchpoints. It's easy to see why; work touchpoints are obvious—they are the repeated steps you take to deliver what a client is paying you for. But the work touchpoints are only half of the CX equation. The second half, which covers the relationship touchpoints, is where you can truly foster connection.

Relationship Touchpoints

Most people overlook relationship touchpoints when they think about the client experience. That's unfortunate because these touchpoints are extremely valuable. Fortunately, that doesn't have to be the case for you; you will learn how to master the relationship touchpoints and then use them to generate referrals from your clients. Your success is, in fact, grounded in your ability to execute on relationship touchpoints.

Consider, as an example, the difference it makes in the relationship with a client when an architect writes a thank-you note and mails it to welcome a new client or when an interior designer finishes the design and installation of the house renovation and sends a "loved working with you" gift of gratitude.

To evoke the emotions you want from your clients—love— you must have an intentional and repeatable outreach you can use to build relationships. By packaging your client experience through a series of relationship-building touchpoints, you can really turn your clients into raving, loyal fans. Then you can extend the value of some of those relationship touchpoints to generate referrals.

Now, don't misunderstand—the work you do and the results it produces for your clients matter significantly. But when people talk about a company they love, they always share how the business makes them *feel* in addition to the results they have.

What's the difference? The work touchpoints and the relationship touchpoints both evoke emotions, but the emotions are different on each side of the formula.

The work touchpoints typically evoke logical and fact-based emotions (though not always, depending on how you help your clients). What does this sound like? Comments like "job done well," "on time," "on budget," and "achieved the desired results." While good, these fact-based reactions can be pretty cut-and-dry. The relationship touchpoints, on the other hand, evoke emotions like feeling cared for, seen, or even indulged. What does this sound like? Comments like "I knew I was more than just a number," or "They surprised me with their care and genuineness." These touchpoints make it clear to the client that they matter more to you than just revenue in your bank account.

You want to do awesome, amazing work for your clients— and you want to build a relationship with them that fosters loyalty and connection. A strong, intentional client experience that makes clients *proud* to be your clients delivers on both parts of the formula: the work touchpoints and the relationship touchpoints. You must have both.

A strong, intentional client experience that makes clients *proud* to be your clients delivers on both parts of the formula: the work touchpoints and the relationship touchpoints. You must have both.

Touchpoint Considerations

At this point, I'm sure you are starting to consider what you currently offer as the touchpoints in your client experience. The first to come to mind are typically the work touchpoints—the letter of agreement or contract clients sign, the website you build, the financial statements you send after you've reconciled the books, the mood board you present as part of the design phase.

Each business has several touchpoints it executes on to get the work done. The list might be quite long, in fact, but what matters more than that, as you move further into creating an excellent all-around client experience, is actually the ratio of work touchpoints to relationship touchpoints.

How you balance that ratio matters; you don't want to overwhelm your client with double the number of relationship touchpoints relative to the work. Add in too many relationship touchpoints, and it feels overdone and fake, like you are trying too hard. Use too few, and your efforts may go unnoticed and unrecognized as they won't help you maintain positive emotions throughout all three stages of a client's work with you. So, what to do? In my experience, business owners benefit the most by ensuring that 25 to 30 percent of all touchpoints are relationship-based touchpoints, so that's what you should aim for.

Of course, I don't advocate for using just any old relationship touchpoints; it's important to create the right ones at the right times based on the emotion that each stage of the client experience evokes in your clients. As we move through the three client stages in part 2, I'll explain more about how and why you can create the right relationship-based touchpoints. For now, the key thing to remember is that maintaining connection with clients is just as important as doing excellent and quality work.

Mapping Out Your Current CX

Before exploring the specifics of where you want to go with your client experience, it's time to take a step back and assess what you are doing currently. It might be tempting to focus on the CX you wish you had and plan to build after you finish reading this book. But you can't skip the first step to getting where you want to go: recognizing where you're starting from. What do you actually have happening in your business right now? What does your current client experience look like, and what would I experience if I hired you today?

Since people have different preferences for how to map out their current client experience, I give my clients three options that I've found to be most effective: the bullet-point format, the mind-mapping method, and the timeline approach. They all work well; which one you choose is simply personal preference. Do you see things visually? Draw it out using the mind-mapping technique. If, instead, you imagine things linearly, with a start and end, use the timeline technique. If you tend to think in ordered lists, use the bullet-point approach.

I find that no matter how you eventually map out your client experience, you will start by just taking notes as you think through what you do; this is why the bullet-point approach is often the best starting point and the one I'll concentrate on here. (The workbook covers all three.)

To start, I invite you to answer the questions listed below. This exercise will help you begin thinking about the work and relationship touchpoints that you currently have and to look closely at what already exists. Working from your current touchpoints, you will begin to see what's missing. Once you've identified the gaps, it's much easier to tweak or adjust the approach.

Please don't worry if you start this exercise feeling that you don't do enough—or any—relationship-building touchpoints. You are far from alone, and the framework this book provides will solve that for you as you move through each section. (The companion workbook outlines these with additional prompts and space to write your answers.)

To jump-start this process, answer these questions first: What is the one event that happens right after a client says yes to working with you? When they say yes to you, do you send an agreement to be signed, do you send a calendar invite for a first client meeting, or do they sign up or register with you through an online form?

Doing this exercise is easier if you think of one of your more recent clients who just started or possibly finished with you. Answer these questions below, and bullet point out your answers as you go. Next, arrange your bullet points in order, from start to finish and from the new to the active to the alumni (if you have one) client stages.

This exercise is useful because it gets you thinking about your client's steps. But please know I'm not looking for perfection. You'll probably miss a detail or two right now, but there will be time to finalize this coming up, so don't overthink it. Just focus on providing a good, rough outline of the work and relationship touchpoints that make up your current client experience.

Ready? Here are the questions. (If you're using the workbook, these questions are included along with a few additional ones.)

- What is the one event that happens right after a client says yes to working with you?

- After your client said yes, and you delivered your first touchpoint (maybe a contract or agreement delivered to be signed), what happened next?

- How do you communicate as you move forward?

- Do you follow up with information in an email?

- Do you schedule meetings, or will you schedule a series of meetings?

- Is there paperwork to be completed and, if so, by whom?

- What information do you need to gather from the client?

- How do you deliver the work?

- What are the phases of work you do?

- How or when do you communicate as you move further along in the client engagement?

- What happens when the work is finished? Or is the work never finished, and parts of the work you do start over every year or month?

- Do you deliver any client appreciation touchpoints, maybe a holiday card? Or do you host a client appreciation event?

I want to emphasize again that it's important to complete this step with what you are *currently doing,* no matter how tempting it is to look ahead. Please don't include what you wish you were doing, plan to do, or sometimes do when time allows or when you remember. Only write down what you actually do for every client now, even if it's a bare minimum. And remember, this exercise is just for you; a rough outline is fine.

Digital Downloads: Find the additional resources mentioned in this chapter on our reader-only resource page at referableclientexperience.com/insider-resources.

3

What a Client Feels Matters Most

C AN YOU DO ME A FAVOR? Can you take a moment and look back over the client experience you just mapped out? Now, pat yourself on the back. I know, corny, right? But most will get to this step and blow past the exercise and then wonder why they struggle to put the rest of what I'm going to teach in place.

As a business owner, you know it is always easier to edit from what's already been written, to duplicate a template that already exists, versus trying to start from scratch. You can use the same approach here by adding to and elevating your client experience from your existing client workflow. This approach is not only easier, it also helps you more quickly identify how and where you can put new touchpoints in place once you determine how you want your clients to feel when working with you.

What *Should* Your Clients Feel?

Did you know that you don't have to leave how your clients feel to chance? You can be intentional by choosing just a few touchpoints to impact how they feel about you. To know which touchpoints to include, you first need to decide what you want your clients to feel when working with you. Those feelings or reactions will form what I call "Ideal Client Reactions." With this knowledge, you'll be able to decide what you'll do—the touchpoints—to evoke those emotions.

To get you started, I'm going to walk you through an exercise. (If you have the workbook, please use the step-by-step framework included to make this exercise easier.)

First up: Consider some service providers you have hired lately. Write down the company name and what you hired them for. Now jot down what you thought or how you felt as you were making the decision to hire them and through the completion of the work. Think back to the initial conversation you had with them, what you thought after you said yes to their services, and what you considered after you started working with them. Think about which service providers made you feel confident and positive about your decision and which you were unsure about and found concern or doubt starting to creep in.

Now, let's look even closer at those you felt confident with. What was it, exactly, about the experience that made you happy, that left you feeling satisfied or confident? Was it that you knew what to expect? Did they have over-the-top communication? Were you pleasantly surprised in any way throughout that process? Did they treat you like you were important? If something did go wrong, did they fix it right away, which kept your confidence intact?

Remember, what you hired the company to fix or solve for you is irrelevant; what's most important is how you felt and what made you feel that way. Write down as much as you can about your feelings and what the business was doing to evoke those feelings. For example, one of my clients who had hired a professional service provider wrote, "The communication was locked in. They repeated themselves just enough to not be annoying, but so I knew what to expect and what was expected from me."

Next, think about when you felt concerned or had doubts after hiring a company. What led to your concern? Did something not go as well as you thought it would or not play out the way you anticipated? Were you left in the dark, wondering what would come next? Did you feel that what you needed to do to not hold up the process wasn't clearly articulated to you? Did they say they would get back to you and then didn't so you had to follow up? What made this experience a negative one? Ask yourself, "What went wrong?" Did they have sloppy or choppy communication? Did they leave something undone? Did they not finish the job? Or did they not finish the job in the way you thought they would? How did you feel you were treated? I'm sure you've had a few experiences where you signed on the dotted line to engage with a service provider and then felt like they disappeared, right? Write down your answers to these questions.

Keep in mind, I'm not talking about identifying the perfect experience from the perfect company so you can become perfect yourself. No one is perfect, which is fine. You don't need to be perfect to make clients happy and loyal. Rational clients don't expect you to be perfect all the time. What I want you to do here is look critically at those businesses where the experience went well and those where it just didn't.

Doing this exercise, and considering how you reacted to other company experiences, can reveal some common themes that you want to duplicate or avoid. Maybe this exercise helps you realize how important the onboarding process is to making your clients feel like they are in good hands. Or maybe you see differently how the lulls in the work you do can cause angst for clients wondering what is going on. Make sure to write these thoughts down as they will all go into informing how you want to improve and elevate your client experience.

Now, take a moment to review what you've written down. How you felt working with other companies when you were the client will inform the feelings and emotions you want to evoke from your clients when they work with you. Those feelings you want to evoke will be determined with this next exercise, the Ideal Client Reaction.

Determining Your Ideal Client Reaction

While the following exercise, determining your Ideal Client Reaction, may seem simple, it is not one to take lightly. It can actually be quite powerful because having your Ideal Client Reaction script in front of you gives you a consistent grounding point to use when you start tweaking your own client experience. Keep your findings handy; you will need to come back to this Ideal Client Reaction activity when it's time to decide what to include in your client experience. It not only provides a base from which to choose the reactions you want your clients to have, but it also reinforces your direction and purpose as you build your client experience.

To complete this activity, I invite you to write down the feelings you *want* your clients to feel about you along with how they might then describe you. Write down the words that describe how you want your clients to feel about working with you and your team (if you have one). Words and phrases I have seen companies come up with over the years have included "special," "seen," "feeling cared for," "being wowed," "true partnership," and "unshakable confidence." Feel free to brainstorm here; there isn't a limit to the list—just write it all down. You won't use everything you write down in your final Ideal Client Reaction script, but having a variety of options to pull from will help you identify possible reactions. From there, you can then narrow those down to the most important ones. (If you are using the workbook, there is a place for your Ideal Client Reaction brain dump.)

For those thinking about skipping this step, please know this activity is an important piece of the process because, as you build your client experience, you need to keep these reactions in mind. Doing so keeps your focus on fostering connection and providing an experience that builds the groundwork for your clients to want to refer new clients to you.

Again, don't skip creating your Ideal Client Reaction script; it is valuable. If you are having trouble coming up with your ideal reactions, let's look at some from my clients who have completed this exercise.

Ideal Client Reaction Script Examples

Eryn Morgan is a business coach for creative business owners, most of whom became business owners accidentally. They are great graphic designers, website designers, copywriters, or photographers. She coaches them on growing their business, while streamlining how they run it. When she completed the Ideal Client Reaction activity, she landed on these four reactions:

- Wicked Smart,
- Commitment to Success,
- Supported Throughout the Process,
- Had My Back.

Randall Brody is the founder of Tax Samaritan, a company that focuses on helping expats living abroad file and handle their taxes and helps those needing assistance in dealing with tax issues with the IRS. Randall decided these three reactions serve his client experience best:

- **D-D Reaction:** Feels that we were Determined to Deliver. We are knowledgeable and disciplined about providing insane experiences with simplicity and integrity.

- **E-E Reaction:** Feels that we were Eager to Engage. We are informative and respond in a timely fashion with relevant, effective communication.

- **H-H Reaction:** Feels that we were Happy to Help. We are compassionate, helpful, and treasure relationships (just like a Samaritan).

Eryn and Randall have very different types of businesses serving different types of clients, and yet both of them were able to use the Ideal Client Reaction activity to narrow down how they wanted their clients to feel. I expect the same will be true for you; you'll see evidence that the experience is working revealed in the reactions you hear from your clients.

I firmly believe that you should intentionally curate client experience reactions; there's really no reason to leave them up to chance. My Ideal Client Reaction script includes the following:

- My clients feel seen and heard.

- My clients feel supported with strategies that are authentic for them.

- My clients trust the process and me.

Your Turn: Finalizing Your Ideal Client Reaction Script

When building out your Ideal Client Reaction, aim to land somewhere between three to four reactions. Having too few minimizes this process, and having too many can make it hard to wrangle everything into your client experience when you start to build it. While it can be challenging to pick and choose, it is an important step. (When writing these down, I encourage you to use a pencil until you commit to the reactions you chose.)

You'll need to narrow down the brainstorming list of the eight or twelve reactions you made earlier to create a final list of just three to four reactions. Use the examples above to help guide you, but give yourself some space to add your unique and customized stamp on your Ideal Client Reaction script. To see this process unfold, you can download Eryn's complete brainstorming activity from initial brain dump to finalized Ideal Client Reaction script on our reader-only resource page.

As I said at the beginning of this book, it's all about asking the right questions. Here's one to get you started: What have clients said to you in the past about why they like working with you? Use your answer to start brainstorming your Ideal Client

Reaction script. Once you have your final three or four reactions, you can then map those reactions to your current client experience.

I do want to address one concern you may have at this point. No matter how intentional you are with the client experience you are about to build and the emotions you want your clients to have, there will always be those clients who don't seem to have the experience you want for them. That's not on you as the business owner. You might feel responsible, but as long as you repeatedly deliver on an intentional client experience, you have done your job. If the majority of clients react the way you want and provide positive feedback, then you will have to learn to be okay with a small number of clients who don't have the experience you want.

In my experience, I have found when a client doesn't have the experience either of us were hoping they would have, it's because they didn't make time to do their part as the client, failed to stay consistent with what was asked of them, and, in some cases, knew what they were signing up for but hoped it'd be different once they became a client. You can't change the experience of a client like that, no matter how much you wish you could.

Mapping Your Ideal Client Reaction Script to Your Current CX

Now you're going to pull out your current client experience that you mapped out in chapter 2. Look closely and ask yourself: Where, in your current client experience touchpoints, do you believe your clients are having the reactions you identified in your Ideal Client Reaction? Just jot down your thoughts on emotions you believe you evoke as you move through your client experience from start to finish. Notice if any patterns emerge.

When you build your CX with these emotions in mind, you don't leave how your clients feel about you to chance.

Use this as a reflective activity; don't aim to match a reaction to every touchpoint in your CX. Don't get too granular. It may be helpful to think back through what your clients have shared or mentioned in the past when you hit a certain moment while working with them. It's also important to make note of the lack of reactions, particularly if you thought they would have a reaction and they didn't. Jot everything down, the reactions received and the lack of reactions, and start to identify gaps.

The Ideal Client Reaction script serves as a guiding light for what you may add or tweak in your intentional CX when you have finally built it. When you build your CX with these emotions in mind, you don't leave how your clients feel about you to chance. For example, if you want your clients to react with trust, you may look to improve your onboarding and offboarding processes with more communication so you can build and maintain continuous trust with your clients.

With your current CX mapped out and your Ideal Client Reaction script finalized, you are now ready to move onto the next phase of the book, where I will walk you through each stage of the client experience and provide details on how to improve your CX with best practices, how to avoid common pitfalls, and more.

Digital Downloads: Find the additional resources mentioned in this chapter on our reader-only resource page at referableclientexperience.com/insider-resources.

PART 2

CONNECT THE STAGES OF THE CLIENT EXPERIENCE

4

Nail the New Client Stage

"HOW LONG IS THIS GOING TO TAKE?" I groaned to my husband, Norm. "I mean, it's just some paint colors and some fabric, right? Should it really be taking this long?"

As the calm one in our relationship, his response was on point: "I don't know—I'm not an interior designer, nor have I ever been one. Why don't you call her and see what's going on?" Then he added for emphasis, "Maybe your perception is wrong about this process."

He was right—he usually is. It's very annoying. Even after twenty years of marriage, it's still annoying.

The process he was talking about was the process of completing a home renovation and addition; a process we launched one month after we brought our youngest (McKenzie) home from the hospital. It made sense. We needed another bedroom and bathroom to accommodate our growing family; we were feeling the squeeze in our small three-bedroom ranch home. Instead of adding on more kid rooms, we decided to add on a new master suite. Not continuing to share a sink and tiny bathroom with my husband was the deciding factor.

I could imagine the layout of our home addition, but I couldn't figure out how to design it. All I had were a few pictures from home design magazines and curtains from my old office that I wanted to incorporate. I was stuck. I knew I needed help—professional design help. So, I hired an interior designer; we'll call her Sarah.

Sarah's amazing. Truly amazing. I mean, this is the interior designer who convinced me to put black carpet in my master bedroom. Genius. I loved it. Every single day that I walked into my bedroom, I loved it.

But when I first hired her, I didn't appreciate just how amazing she would be. Our work together got off to a bit of a rocky start.

At first, everything seemed wonderful. When I reached out to her for help with my master suite, she was communicative and friendly. Our first meeting was great—she listened very well, understood what I was going for, and set off to design an amazing space for my husband and me.

Then, crickets.

Days turned into two weeks without me hearing anything. I started grumbling, at least internally. "How hard could it be? It's just paint color, some fabric, and a little furniture. Right?"

Actually, no, that wasn't right at all. (And I can hear the snicker from every interior designer reading this book.) But I didn't understand that because Sarah didn't tell me how the magic of creative design works. She didn't set my expectations as to what goes into a great design process.

Without knowing what to expect or the timeline she was working on, I had made my own assumptions about her creative process, how fast it should move, and how easy it would be.

As it turned out, I was wrong. Dead wrong.

But, as an uninformed client, I didn't know that then, and that's where the trouble started.

First Impressions

I'm sure you've heard the cliché that first impressions matter. In the world of client relationships, nothing could be more true. The new client stage is a critical juncture that sets the tone for your entire client relationship. During this time, you need to meet your clients where they are and reassure them that they made the right decision in hiring you.

You could almost consider the new client stage like the honeymoon phase of the client experience. Just as newly-weds use the early months of their marriage to build a strong foundation, you need to use the new client stage to lay the groundwork for a successful client experience.

However, many business owners overlook the importance of this stage, rushing to dive into the work without fully addressing what the client is feeling and thinking. It's easy to fall into the trap of thinking, "They hired us, we're good," but that is far from the full story. Failing to understand this can lead to misunderstandings and unmet expectations—and it can severely reduce the chances that the client becomes a raving fan and a referring client. In your eagerness to start the client work, you need to remember a crucial fact: Even after they've decided to hire you, new clients have a strong desire to reestablish trust with—and credibility in—you.

The moment a client signs on with you, they enter a vulnerable state. They've made a significant investment—of money, time, and trust—and this can trigger what psychologists call "post-decision dissonance." In common parlance, this is referred to as "buyer's remorse." This is a period of uncertainty when the client may question their decision, wonder if they've made the right choice, or worry about the potential outcomes.

If you ignore these underlying thoughts and concerns and jump straight into doing the work for your clients, you miss a crucial opportunity to reinforce the client's decision, connect at a deeper level, and build a stronger foundation for the client experience. As best as you can, you should try not to leave a client in a state of feeling unsure, anxious, or even regretful about their choice to work with you. Think about your Ideal Client Reaction script. Make sure that you have addressed how crucial it is at the new client stage to take care of what you want the client to feel.

High Stakes

The new client stage has high stakes. You know how hard—even painful—it can be to bring on a new client, so the last thing you want to do after securing a new client is to lose them. But the chances of that happening in the new client stage are higher than many realize. Research conducted by Design Symphony, a consultancy firm, revealed a startling statistic: Businesses can lose anywhere from 20 to 80 percent of new clients within the first hundred days of engagement. This staggering figure underscores the critical nature of the new client stage and the need for a targeted approach to overcome subconscious buyer's remorse.

Buyer's remorse, or post-decision anxiety, is not a reflection on your skills or the value you provide. It's a natural psychological phenomenon that occurs when people make significant decisions or investments. The key is to recognize it and address it head-on.

If left unaddressed, this anxiety can:

1. Erode trust before you've had a chance to fully establish it,
2. Lead to miscommunication and misaligned expectations,
3. Damage your reputation through negative word of mouth,
4. Reduce the likelihood of referrals and repeat business.

While you need to make sure you have touchpoints in place to overcome buyer's remorse, you also have an opportunity in this stage to build on the excitement the client felt when they first said yes to working with you. Think about it: When you decide to engage with a new vendor or company for your business, you feel encouraged as you anticipate finding the solution to solve your problem. Your clients feel the same about you. Having strong touchpoints during the new client stage helps you make the most of this exciting time as your clients start their journey. Overcoming buyer's remorse means you remind your clients they made the right choice and help them feel calmer. At the same time, you fire them up with excitement to work with you. This allows you to move your clients from just satisfied clients to raving fans. And from raving fans, you have the greatest potential to unlock the flow of referrals.

Addressing the Quiet Voice

The key to successfully navigating the new client stage lies in acknowledging and addressing what I call the "quiet voice"— those unspoken concerns and doubts that clients may be hesitant to express directly. By proactively speaking to these concerns, without your client ever having to bring them up, you can alleviate anxiety, build trust, and set the stage for a productive and positive working relationship. It's like being inside your client's head, knowing what they are thinking, and being willing to call out the elephant in the room. One way to do this is by carefully wording your welcome card to make sure you address concerns and go beyond generic welcome language.

For example, when I was a business and productivity coach, I specifically wrote the welcome card I mailed to clients after they entered the new client stage to acknowledge that our coaching sessions could be hard and that the process could stretch them and ask them to make tough choices. The point of my welcome card was to weave in that language to acknowledge how they are feeling and to make sure they knew that I understood their emotions as well. Here is the language I used:

> Thank you for the opportunity to work together. This journey may stretch and challenge you, but you're not on this journey alone. I'm your copilot, and I'm here to help you every step of the way.

This language is very different from the typical welcome-card language that speaks only about how happy you are that they are a client. Think of generic language like "Thank you for coming on board" or "We're excited to dive in and work with you."

Another option to address that quiet voice is a welcome gift, which, like the welcome card, is designed to acknowledge that emotions may run high while working with you and to communicate that they are in excellent hands. When working with one of my clients who was looking to put together a gift to clients who were planning to buy a business, the first question I asked him was, "What are they feeling at this point in their journey, and how can you support them through the items you add in the gift box?" You have to put yourself in your clients' shoes first. No one needs another coffee mug or a box of chocolates, unless it meets a need of what they are feeling. (For more examples, visit the reader-only resource page.)

One of my absolute, all-time favorite ways to address the quiet voice is to visually show your clients the process that lies ahead. I call it the "Expectation Map," as in mapping out what the client can expect while working with you. An Expectation Map lays out a step-by-step representation of the client journey from start to finish. It's a powerful tool that can provide clarity on the process. As the client sees each part of the process unfold before them on the page, their expectations begin to realign. In this setting, you might also provide time ranges to set realistic expectations for how long a phase or point in the process usually takes and highlight how the process might slow down if you meet a challenge beyond your control or if the client delays providing information you might need to move forward. Finally, seeing the process visually on paper gives your clients a sense of control.

Had I understood what was happening and how long it would take to hear from Sarah after our initial interior design meeting, I would have confidently waited to hear from her, rather than getting upset and concerned.

Expectation Mapping

Here's an overview of how to create an effective Expectation Map. Keep in mind, this is a different process than the one I walked you through in chapter 2 when I asked you to map out the work and relationship touchpoints you do that are contained in the totality of your client experience. This map

As the client sees each part of the process unfold before them on the page, their expectations begin to realign.

is higher level and addresses how a client would see working with you. Your client experience includes many behind-the-scenes to-dos and touchpoints that your clients never see. What they see on the map is the process of working with you unfolding. Here's how to do it.

1   Outline or map out your typical client engagement into clear, distinct phases. I find it easier to draw this out. One suggestion is to pretend you are talking to a prospect and walk them through your process, drawing it out as you go. I did this in real time for a photographer once, and it looked like a child had connected a few dots with some straight lines. The dots represented what the client could expect, in order, and the connecting lines from one dot to another showed the direction of movement and the length of time between the dots. I thought about including this drawing in the book so that you could truly appreciate how bad it was, but I'm not sure I could handle the snickering from my teenagers when they spot it. (You can take a peek at it on our reader-only resource page.)

2   Focus on identifying key milestones—not every little detail or every single deliverable—and group them so your map has a few sections or phases. Some common phases are the onboarding phase, the delivery phase, and the wrap-up phase. For example, a milestone an attorney might include in the onboarding phase would be the letter of agreement that the client needs to sign and return. A milestone a web-site designer might include in the delivery phase could be the presentation of the website, along with the acknowl-edgment of two rounds of editing.

3   Make sure to address common concerns, like routine questions you get, how long a phase could take, or what could derail the timetable. You may be able to add these items right onto your map or mention them when you present the Expectation Map to your clients and walk them through the particular phases.

4   Highlight the client's responsibilities by making it clear what action they will need to take, like providing information, completing a document, or providing feedback. Don't forget to mention how their effort, or lack thereof, could—or will—delay the timetable of completing the work for them. If you can't build or finalize your client's new website without their new headshots and lifestyle images, you need to remind them of that.

5   Now make it visual: Create a graphic representation of your client journey. This could be a timeline, a roadmap, or even a board-game layout. I tell my clients to think about the map like the board from Candy Land or Monopoly.

Seeing an Expectation Map visually helps connect the dots to what this map is ultimately trying to accomplish. Here's an abbreviated example of a client's Expectation Map. We zoomed in on one section for the purpose of legibility, but you can view the full version of the map on the reader-only resource page.

Lauren's map is one of my favorite Expectation Maps. When she was a business coach, she worked with clients to help them navigate the process of buying a franchise. Using her map allowed her to talk openly about what a client would feel at certain points in the process of working with her. With it, she could position reactions and feelings her clients were having as

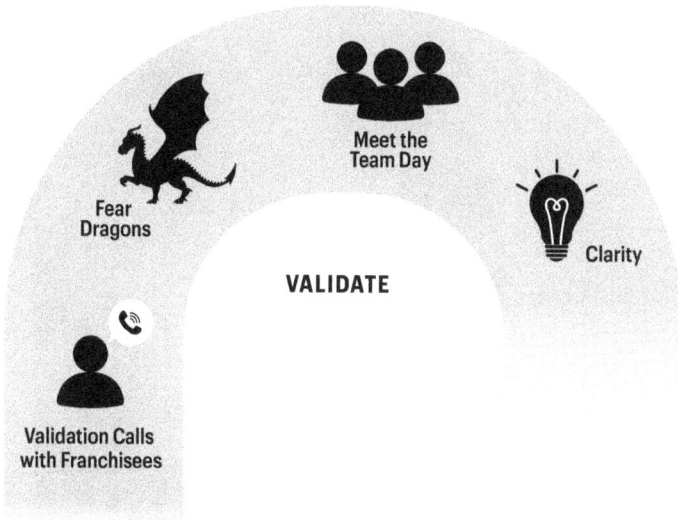

Expectation Map Example 1: The Road Ahead by Lauren Cantor

normal because they were expected. Her use of the "fear drag-ons" imagery allowed her to address head-on any fear and the emotional roller coaster her clients might feel going through the process of deciding to buy a business. By including these emotions, she removed their stigma and normalized them.

To give you another Expectation Map option, I'm including in this chapter the map I share with clients when they join my referral coaching program. To make sure they see it, I place it on the "Thank You" page they see after they officially regis-ter, add it to their client Google Drive folder for easy access, and review it during their one-on-one onboarding call with me. The map helps me talk through the importance of the first ninety-day sprint that we create together and the value of them advocating for what they need next based on their first ninety days in the program. I also walk through the map with

The Journey to Building Your Referrable Business

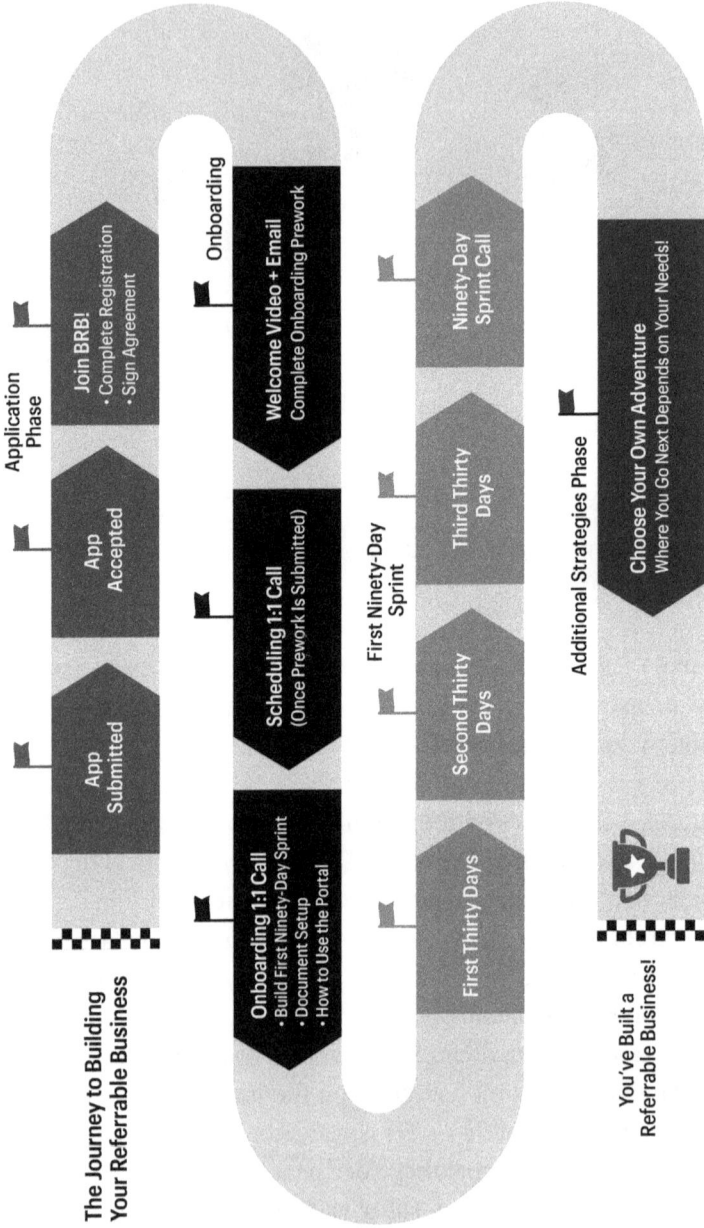

Application Phase

- **App Submitted**
- **App Accepted**
- **Join BRB!**
  - Complete Registration
  - Sign Agreement

Onboarding

- **Onboarding 1:1 Call**
  - Build First Ninety-Day Sprint
  - Document Setup
  - How to Use the Portal
- **Scheduling 1:1 Call**
  - (Once Prework Is Submitted)
- **Welcome Video + Email**
  - Complete Onboarding Prework

First Ninety-Day Sprint

- **First Thirty Days**
- **Second Thirty Days**
- **Third Thirty Days**
- **Ninety-Day Sprint Call**

Additional Strategies Phase

- **Choose Your Own Adventure**
  - Where You Go Next Depends on Your Needs!

You've Built a Referrable Business!

Expectation Map Example 2: What to Expect by Stacey Brown Randall prospects in the buyer's journey to help them see what they are buying, so to speak.

By providing such a visual guide, you're not just telling clients what to expect—you're showing them. This tangible representation of their journey can significantly reduce anxiety and build excitement for the process ahead.

(In the workbook, you'll find pages where you can draw or bullet point out your Expectation Map. I have also included other samples of my clients' Expectation Maps on this book's reader-only resource page.)

Getting the New Client Stage Right

In chapter 2, I provided you with a quick overview of the new client stage. Let's take a quick review before you take a deeper dive.

Essentially, the new client stage begins the moment the client decides to work with you. As they exit the buyer's journey, they take their first step into your client experience and enter the new client stage. When the new client stage ends depends on the workflow within your business. Remember, when the new client stage ends, it is because your client is entering the next stage—the active or ongoing client stage.

Now is a great time to look back at the client experience mapping you did in chapter 2 and mark when your new client stage ends. Typically, the end date of the new client stage is dictated by an action the client takes, not necessarily a date on the calendar. When I was a business and productivity coach, the end of my new client stage was the first coaching session. The new client stage ran from the point they said yes to working with me, signed their coaching agreement, and confirmed their recurring appointment times; it continued through the end of their first coaching session. For some clients, that lasted only thirty days, and for others, a few months, depending on when they scheduled their first coaching appointment.

While this stage is typically shorter than the other two stages, there isn't an industry standard that you have to follow. Remember, the ending of the new client stage is completely subjective—you decide when you want to declare the new client stage as over. After you put everything you've learned from this book into place and start testing out the boundary of the new client stage with a few new clients, you may even change your mind.

For some, this contextual definition is liberating. For others, the uncertainty makes the decision feel hard. If you are struggling to decide when your new client stage ends, answering this question might make it easier: At what point does a client no longer feel new to me? With all the clients you've worked with before, at what point would you say the client has moved into the getting-the-work-done step and the newness has worn off? For example, an estate planning attorney could determine the new client stage ends after the client returns all the documentation needed to draft an estate plan. The new client stage ends with them uploading or emailing the requested documents, which allows the attorney to start working on drafting the legal documents. (To provide you with additional help working through this, I have included a few more prompting questions in the workbook.)

Visualize Your Start and End Points

Answering the following two questions right now will help you visualize your starting and ending touchpoints. First: What is the first step or action a client takes when they say yes to working with you? For my business, one way a client can work with me is through my VIP Experience program. The first step that a prospect takes to become a VIP client is to confirm their VIP dates (these are the dates I'll travel to their office to teach and implement the multilayered referral strategy I built for their team). Once we enter their VIP dates into our system, we send the new client their registration form to complete.

The second question you need to ask yourself: What is the *last* touchpoint of the new client stage? For me, the last touchpoint in the new client stage for a VIP Experience client is when I return to the office after completing their two in-person days, and I deliver their twelve-month deployment roadmap of how to implement everything we just built together, broken down by month and who is responsible.

Keep in mind that the end point you pick right now may shift over time as you pull the entire client experience together and make necessary adjustments.

Avoiding Common Pitfalls

Between the starting and ending touchpoints of the new client stage, a lot can happen. In this section, we'll look at some common pitfalls to avoid so you can decide if you need to add additional touchpoints within this stage.

First, I recommend establishing your communication preferences as early as possible. If you like to respond to clients by email and not text message, let them know. Clarifying your preferred communication methods, whether that is email, phone, or messaging apps like Slack, also provides you with the opportunity to set expectations for response times and when you will be scheduling regular check-ins or progress updates.

Second, make it clear who your clients can, and should, reach out to for different needs. Often, the business owner is not the best first person to ask. I heard a business owner explain it this way: He wanted his clients to go to someone who was "better than me." He had hired people to be the best at certain parts of the business, and he wanted his clients to know that and feel comfortable going straight to the right team member.

For clients to do this comfortably, you'll need to make sure to introduce your team members. You can introduce them via email by explaining who everyone is and when clients might need to reach out to them. Include their contact information as well. You can also do this in a printed brochure or a video introduction.

By establishing your communication channels and the team your clients will be working with as early as possible, you limit the chances that your clients will experience confusion or frustration. In other words, you make the work easier to complete. But remember, your goal isn't just to start work—it's to start a relationship. By investing time and effort into this crucial stage, you're not just retaining clients by overcoming buyer's remorse and delivering high-quality work; you're deepening the connection and relationship so you create advocates right from the beginning who will drive your business forward.

Digital Downloads: Find the additional resources mentioned in this chapter on our reader-only resource page at referableclientexperience.com/insider-resources.

5

Master the Active Client Stage

AFTER THE EXCITEMENT of onboarding a new client wears off, you move into a period when you do roughly the same thing for each client. Most of the work gets delivered in this time frame, otherwise known as the active client stage. For some, this stage can be long, very long. There is usually a flow of client work, and the "what to do" and in "what order to do it" becomes pretty much routine.

Working from a checklist of some sort helps keep the routine moving forward seamlessly, because forgetting just once to do a routine step for a client will push you to figure out how not to end up in that position again. Take it from me. I'll never forget the night I sat straight up in bed, jolted awake by the sinking feeling that I had forgotten to do something for a client. This hadn't been a one-off request; it was part of the regular deliverables within my client experience. It was something that all my clients usually received, but I had let it slip, mostly because I was relying on memory to do it.

I got out of my warm bed and headed for the kitchen, where my laptop was. My face all aglow from the computer screen in the dark, cold kitchen, I emailed the deliverable to my client.

Phew. Then I headed back to bed, though I was already wide awake with my mind racing in a million different directions. What else had I missed? How was the client going to react or feel after receiving this deliverable in the middle of the night? How could I keep this midnight jolt from ever returning? I am sure, as a fellow business owner, you can relate.

My solution to my middle-of-the-night jolt was to map out—in writing—the touchpoints I executed on for my clients. It wasn't pretty, just sketched out in bullet points on a piece of paper (like I walked you through in chapter 2). Later, I added those into a project management software-as-a-service (SaaS) tool (Process Street was the one I chose at the time), allowing the software to send me reminders of what to do next, so the software could take the lead in remembering what I needed to execute on and when.

What I'm saying here is that you have to write it down. Mapping out all the to-dos within your client experience—the individual work and relationship touchpoints—only works if you put it in black and white. I know I'm repeating myself here; it's just that, for some reason, some business owners resist taking the time to do this step. But not you, right? I am no longer surprised when business owners show me their half-done checklists of what they do for their clients, refer vaguely to some digital documents collecting dust, or just plain old leave it up to their memory. Which, let's be honest, after forty, is a dangerous solution.

Please also note, this mapping out of your entire client experience is very different from the Expectation Map you created for your new client stage touchpoint. The Expectation Map is a high-level view from the client's perspective. Now, you're getting specific about the behind-the-scenes work you do. You're writing down all of the touchpoints that you do for clients within each of the three stages, leaving nothing out, and including all the work a client will never see. Again, if you did this in chapter 2, you're ahead of the game. Pull out your list and add anything you might have forgotten or overlooked as you read through this chapter.

When I shared my process of mapping out the client experience from start to finish within the three stages with my client Jackie Ho, a brilliant architect and founder of the boutique architectural firm Ho & Lacy Architecture, she quickly locked in on the value of seeing the work she does for her clients in visual form. She thought it could solve one pressing issue she faced as an architect—dealing with permits and zoning processes in the city of San Francisco. She knew that once a client was in the active client stage with her, they would be there for a while. Here was a predictable pain point she could improve, or even avoid, by drilling down into the active client stage and creating a master checklist for managing her client experience.

Jackie ultimately mapped out her client experience touch-points in a spreadsheet, and it really was a thing of beauty—the headers, the columns, the color coding. You could easily identify which touchpoints went in which stage, and that visibility allowed her to keep the million small, but not insignificant, details for each project locked and loaded so nothing fell through the cracks, no matter how long the active client stage dragged on. The detail really helped her manage the complexity and extended length of this stage for her workflow.

Because that's the main challenge for most when it comes to the active client stage: It's detailed, it can be lengthy, most of the work happens in this stage, and not just for one client at a time. Most business owners have multiple client experiences happening at the same time, and some operate at a different pace than others. It's a recipe for confusion.

By maintaining engagement throughout the active client stage, you set the foundation for future collaborations and provide opportunities to use the right language to generate referrals.

I cannot stress enough the importance of mapping out your current client experience, including all of your work touchpoints, so you can create a checklist, visual map, or timeline of what you do. Doing so enables even the most complex client experience to become automatic. But equally important is that we continue together in this book. Why? I'm about to show you how to layer in relationship touchpoints and figure out how to leverage those moments for referrals. This can only be done with precision once you know your stages and have them mapped out.

Why the Active Client Stage Matters

Because the active client stage of your client experience is when you find yourself delivering the majority of the work, this is where your expertise truly shines. But remember, the quality of your work alone will not keep clients happy. The real challenge lies in keeping the client engaged and connected beyond the work itself, even as that work winds down.

This stage matters because it's where the initial excitement of working with you can wane if you don't carefully nurture it. It's in this phase that you have the opportunity to not only delight your clients with your value but also nurture the relationship into one that lasts past the work that you do. By maintaining engagement throughout the active client stage, you set the foundation for future collaborations and provide opportunities to use the right language to generate referrals.

The active client stage is a critical time for deepening trust, preventing problems, educating the client, and building connections to cultivate referrals. In this stage, you can reinforce and deepen the trust you established in your new client stage as you continue to provide your clients with consistent engagement.

Regular communication allows you to stay connected and helps you identify and address potential issues before they become significant problems. After forty-five days, I send a check-in email after a client has joined my coaching program. In it, I ask the client to share with me which trainings they have completed, what strategy or tactics they have implemented, and where they are getting stuck. For those who respond, I can spot any small issue or confusion and fix it right away before it grows into a larger problem, which becomes harder to overcome at later stages. Getting this conversation started also allows me to follow up and provide any additional direction, resources, or clarity the client might need.

Communication improves client engagement as well, which is important because engaged clients see what you do more regularly, and thus they better understand and appreciate the complexities of your work, leading to more realistic expectations and greater satisfaction. Plus, when you mix in relationship-based touchpoints, you have the opportunity to use language, called "referral seeds," to cultivate referrals. There is more coming up in later chapters about referral seeds, but, for now, just know they are how you add a little fuel to the fire to generate referrals from your clients.

When you're doing the work, it's easy to fall back into the trap of thinking that the work constitutes the most important connection points with your clients, especially when the project goes on for a long time. Many businesses produce an immense amount of work behind the scenes, work the client never sees, so it's natural to consider ways to leverage that work as the sole focus of the active client stage. But depending on product delivery alone limits what is possible with this stage. Crucially, it overlooks critical aspects of the client relationship—the emotional and psychological components of the client experience.

The risks associated with focusing solely on the work itself can be high. By doing this, you risk losing the personal connection you established in the new client stage, those weeks when you provide a lot of one-on-one attention, and your outreach is more intentional. You'll never get that new client energy back. But, by stepping back from the work to check in, you can make sure you don't miss upcoming opportunities, such as addressing evolving client needs or concerns. Additionally, you won't overlook chances to add value beyond the scope of the project that would only be revealed through communication beyond the deliverables.

The truth is, neglecting to build a relationship can have a long-term impact on receiving referrals and getting clients who come back around to work with you again. Don't fall for the assumption that good work speaks for itself. While quality is crucial, it's the ongoing engagement and demonstration of care that truly set you apart, endearing you to your clients.

The Dangers of Complacency

As the excitement of bringing on a new client fades and the day-to-day work takes over, complacency can set in. This complacency is dangerous because it can lead you to take a transactional rather than a relationship-based approach to your clients. Even if the quality of the work you produce is high, the connection and positive emotions your clients feel toward you can decrease, ultimately leading to decreased client retention.

Complacency rears its ugly head in most industries—the longer your clients are with you, the more you risk losing them to a competitor who woos them away when you're not paying enough attention. And you certainly won't receive any ongoing referrals from clients you are neglecting.

Instead, what you want to focus on is increasing client retention. A study by Bain & Company found that increasing client retention rates by just 5 percent can increase profits by 95 percent. Remember, in today's competitive business landscape, delivering great work is the baseline expectation. To truly stand out and create loyal, referring clients, you need to go above and beyond. Let's look at how to infuse the relationship side into the active client stage.

Relationship-Building in the Active Client Stage

To begin integrating relationship-building during this stage, you first need to know which type of active client stage you have. Think back to chapter 2, which broke down the active client stage into two types: the end date and ongoing. The end date refers to an active client stage that ends when the client work is done and has a clear end point. Ongoing refers to an active client stage that doesn't end because you continue to work with your clients year after year. (If you are using the companion workbook, this section is mapped out in a question-by-question format.)

End-Point Active Client Stage

If your active client stage has a clear end point, I want you to think about the work touchpoints plus any relationship touchpoints you have in place for your clients. Not surprisingly, the first active client stage touchpoint immediately follows the final touchpoint in the new client stage. The final active client stage touchpoint signifies that the work is complete and the engagement with the client has come to an end.

Since the length of the active client stage can vary widely, some wrap up within months and some extend for years, it's important to map out what this looks like for your business. Before you consider what you'll add to improve your client experience in the active client stage, you need to write down what consistently happens during this stage for your clients.

Like with the new client stage, choose the bookend moments of your active client stage. First, choose the touchpoints that come immediately after your new client stage ends. Then, choose the last thing you do to finalize the work and engagement with a client. For an interior designer, it could be install day or the photoshoot you have after install day. Keep in mind, the last touchpoint you do during the active client stage could be either a work or a relationship touchpoint, or likely a combination.

Let the rough outline of this from chapter 2 guide you now. Depending on how detailed you were when you originally did this activity, determine what you need to add to finalize this exercise of capturing all touchpoints during the active client stage. For example, if you originally wrote down the team meetings you host with the client's team but didn't write down the weekly or monthly check-ins you provide to the client, now is the time to add those details. Don't forget to include any meetings you have with your internal team or the documents or presentations you prepare.

For those with an ending active client stage, having the final touchpoint mapped out gets you ready for the next and final client stage. But if your active client stage does not end—it continues indefinitely or is ongoing—you'll need to look at the active client stage differently.

Ongoing Active Client Stage

Even though your active client stage doesn't end, it still has a clear starting point—the first touchpoint you do that directly follows the ending of the new client stage. Write down which touchpoint happens first after the client moves from new to active. As you start mapping out this stage, think about the repeating patterns you see in your ongoing active client stage.

You'll probably notice some touchpoint cycles that happen regularly, such as work touchpoints you do every week, every month, and every year. You can use those patterns as the guardrails to map out the rest of your active client stage. For example, as a financial advisor, you would write down your monthly calls, quarterly market update emails, or biannual or annual in-person or virtual reviews. Then work backward to identify other work- or relationship-based touchpoints you do in between those repeating touchpoints. Many of my clients tell me that doing this makes planning much easier.

Thinking of the touchpoints you do routinely as guardrails allows you to fill in the blanks so you don't have to create the entire process from scratch. If you were doing this in stages, one option would be to identify the touchpoints you do once a year, then twice a year, then quarterly, then monthly.

Staying with the financial advisor example, when mapping out the yearly touchpoint, you would write down the in-person annual review you do with each client and the communication touchpoints in getting the review scheduled. Next, look at those touchpoints you do biannually. Maybe that is a check-in phone call that you schedule six months after the yearly review. Write down what you do quarterly and finally monthly—for example, your monthly enewsletter to clients on market updates. The goal is to list out the work and relationship touchpoints that happen like clockwork every year as part of your ongoing active client stage. You can review your active client stage touchpoints to identify gaps where other touchpoints are needed. With each time guardrail, you get closer to bringing your client experience into focus.

While mapping out your active client stage is critical to this process, don't forget, your goal is to shape how your client feels while they are working with you. Reference your Ideal Client Reaction script to determine where you have gaps and additional touchpoints you should incorporate. Remember, you need to add in a few relationship touchpoints as part of this process.

Best Practices for the Active Client Stage

Whether you have an end-point or an ongoing active client stage, you can use a few best practices to go above and beyond. Because they focus on strengthening the relationship, these are touchpoints that help you keep the excitement of working with you alive. (Additional ideas are provided on the reader-only resource page.)

Date-Based Touchpoints

Date-based touchpoints are common because they're reliable and add some ease to relationship-building. You might base them on the calendar itself (such as holiday cards sent every December) or the length of time the client has been with you (such as a "Happy Client Anniversary" card sent to a client on their one-year anniversary).

Another way to execute on touchpoints during the active client stage is to combine a relationship and a work touchpoint. For example, a financial advisor who implemented my Referable Client Experience strategy mailed a small box of cookies to her clients in advance of the annual review. The cookies were mailed directly from the cookie company on behalf of the financial advisor and came with a note:

> [Financial Advisor's Name] of [company name] wanted to share a sweet treat in anticipation of your Annual Review. [Assistant's name] will be reaching out to schedule a good time to meet. Enjoy the cookies while you wait!

This relationship touchpoint has a practical purpose: It reminds the client of the annual review and improves the chances they will pay attention to the assistant's email to get it scheduled. Annual reviews can easily be overlooked by busy clients, creating a vacuum in the relationship-building process. And it doesn't hurt that cookies are delicious. The gift not only prompts the action of scheduling but also creates a pleasant experience that helps the client look forward to having the annual review with the advisor. Having this regular touchpoint in place helped the advisor avoid falling into a rhythm of neglect that is an all-too-easy trap to tumble into when you become increasingly focused on bringing in more new clients each year.

Celebration Touchpoints

For those with an end-point active client stage, your final touchpoint of this stage should be a way to celebrate a successful client engagement or project. You might take the client to lunch or coffee or send them a bottle of champagne. Brian

Stevens, the realtor I mentioned earlier in this book, has a drawing made of the home his client is either selling or buying and delivers it to them after moving day.

And while it may seem like celebration touchpoints are only appropriate for ending the active client stage if you have an end date, you can also use them with the ongoing active client stage to commemorate the start of a second year or next round with a client. For example, a CPA who moves into year two of working with a client to prepare and file their taxes could send a celebration basket of goodies to signify the start of the next year of working together.

These best practices are easy to implement if you first consider the rhythm of your active client stage. With a range of options, you can craft a few powerful and intentional touchpoints that will respect your budget as well. But, as with anything you work to improve, they all require time to create and time to execute.

Progress Visualizations

The longer a client is with you, the more necessary it becomes to help them visualize where they are with the progress of the work you are doing with them. Within my referral coaching program, I work with a client for a twelve-month period in which they complete the strategy trainings they need to build a referable business. Because they move through many trainings (some upward of twenty different strategies), and their success only comes once they start to implement, I provide a strategy and skills checklist so they can check off the strategies they have implemented and the skills they now know how to do. The checklist allows them to see—visually—how far they've come and what they still need to accomplish.

Balancing Efficiency and Engagement

While systemizing your touchpoints is crucial for consistency, it's important to strike a balance between efficiency and genuine engagement by avoiding overreliance on automation as you seek greater efficiency. Automation can be a powerful tool in managing the client experience, but it should not come at the expense of personalization and connection. It should enhance, not replace, the personal touch. Here are some guidelines to help you strike the right balance.

Use automation wisely by leveraging it for scheduling, reminders, and basic follow-ups, but ensure that key communications come directly from you or your team. Even when using automated systems, include personalized elements based on client data you have collected. Think of automation as a way to be proactive in your communication and to maintain a baseline of communication, but be ready to engage personally and promptly when clients reach out.

Automation itself also requires some personal attention from time to time. You cannot use it successfully with a set-it-and-forget-it mindset. Instead, you'll need to continually review your automated processes to ensure they're still relevant and effective. Mixing digital with analog touchpoints can create a well-rounded approach that prioritizes high-value interactions.

My company runs on technology, which makes sense because we serve business owners in more than a dozen countries around the world. I deliver the majority of my work to my clients through an online learning platform that is password protected, online meeting apps like Zoom, and a lot of email. So, when I think about how to connect with my clients—during

Automation can be a powerful tool
in managing the client experience,
but it should not come at the expense
of personalization and connection.

all stages but particularly the active client stage—I focus on what I call mass personalization.

"Mass" and "personalization" sound like a contradiction in terms when used together to form a way of operating. But when you use mass personalization correctly, you can leverage technology to send personal messages, delivering personalized connection in a manageable way. For example, your welcome video script may be basically the same for each client, but the message is just for them. As an example of personalization, I always make sure to say my client's first name and anything relevant to them specifically in my welcome message. When they receive a quick personal video, each client knows it comes directly from me to them. Currently, my favorite tech tool to use for mass personal videos is Bonjoro, but there are plenty of other options out in the marketplace. (For more details on how I use Bonjoro in my business, visit the reader-only resource page.)

Of course, these touchpoints still require a time commitment, no matter how advanced the technology, but it's an investment of time I happily make for my clients. Remember, the goal is to use technology to enhance, not replace, the human element of your client relationships.

For the final activity in this chapter, take a moment to jot down any ideas you have about improving your current active client stage within your client experience. You may want to look back a few pages to the active client stage touchpoints you wrote down to help you think through which new touchpoints you should add and where in the active client stage they should go.

In the next chapter, we will move on to the final stage of the client experience—the alumni client stage. If you have an ongoing active client stage, you can skip this chapter if you prefer. But I encourage you to read it as it might trigger other touchpoint ideas you can incorporate in your ongoing active client stage.

Digital Downloads: Find the additional resources mentioned in this chapter on our reader-only resource page at referableclientexperience.com/insider-resources.

6

Extend the Alumni Client Stage

" ARE YOU SURE you want to do this?" my dad asked.

Then my mom chimed in, "I don't know why both of our children are obsessed with buying houses so young." My real estate agent slowly stood up from the couch and left the living room.

After graduating from college, I moved to Charlotte, North Carolina, and, within a year, I was already looking to buy my first home. I had asked my parents to come to Charlotte to look at two condos I had narrowed in on, and I wanted to make an offer on one of them.

"Yes, Dad. This is the one. It's in a safe area, less than a mile from uptown and my work, and I love it," I responded, ignoring my mom's comment. It's one I had heard many times.

"Okay," he said. "Let's get this process started."

He and my mom walked outside, and she turned to him and said, "Our kids are so much smarter than we were at their age." They both laughed, and I became a homeowner at twenty-three years old.

The home-buying process wasn't without a few ups and downs and hiccups, but I felt perfectly supported and guided by my parents and my real estate agent. She was pretty amazing.

And just a few years later, I couldn't remember who she was. To this day, all I can remember is the company she worked for, but not her name or how to contact her. I couldn't refer her if I wanted to.

Why the Alumni Client Stage Matters

Welcome to the final stage of the client experience. This is the stage that people severely under-plan for or don't think about at all. This is typically because you aren't doing any work touchpoints during this phase, so there isn't a natural prompt to stay connected. But here's why you should care more about your alumni client stage: Nobody can refer you if they don't remember you.

If you lose touch with your previous clients, your alumni clients, you may never hear from them again. And what else should you expect? When you don't have a process to stay connected after the work is done, it's all too easy for clients to forget about you, never work with you again, and fail to refer you.

Here's the thing: I know your clients love you. They sing your praises after the renovation is complete, and your work as their interior designer has made theirs the best house on the block. Or they rest easy at night knowing their business is protected because they hired you as their attorney. Or they see their employees working together in a way they haven't in a long time because they invested in your consulting firm to help them with employee engagement.

They really do appreciate you. But humans have the attention span of a goldfish. Okay, while the claim that our attention spans are shorter than that of a goldfish has been disproven, research continues to show our attention spans are actually decreasing. While your clients love you now, there is a pretty good chance they will have a hard time recalling your name later down the road. Harsh reality, I know.

You can prevent this from happening, though, by leveraging the alumni client stage. As a reminder, this stage only happens if you have an end-point active client stage, meaning your active client stage ends when the client work is done, and the client moves into the alumni client stage.

Why "Alumni" Clients?

You can call this stage anything you want—previous client stage, past client stage—but I've found that by labeling my clients who are no longer active clients as alumni, I think of them differently.

We talked earlier about how a college or university uses the term "alumni." The term connects former students to the school, gives them a label that only people who graduated from that school can use, and fosters connection. Alumni tend to take some level of ownership of their school.

What's important here is not that your clients will feel this deeper connection when you start referring to them as alumni clients. They might feel it, or they might not. But *you* will. That is what matters. Labeling them as alumni clients will help you make a deeper connection than if you just thought of them as "past" or "previous" clients. And it follows that you'll then take

Nobody can
refer you if they don't
remember you.

different actions to cultivate a relationship with these alumni long after they stop being a client.

Speaking of "long," you may be wondering how long you need to nurture your alumni, a frequently asked question from my clients. The prospect of long-term alumni relationships can be daunting when you consider the number of clients you have in the alumni client stage now and how many more will be joining them in just the next twelve months. It adds up fast. Before I dive into my solution for how to stay connected to your alumni clients, I'll go over the parameters to consider when deciding on the length of the alumni client stage.

Length of the Alumni Client Stage

The good news? There's no one right way to do this. The length of your alumni client stage is completely situational. Which, yes, means you need to determine how long an alumni client stays in this stage; you should base this decision on a length of time that works best for you and your business.

Let's start by determining when the alumni client stage begins and then tackle the harder part of determining when it ends. The easiest way to do this is by writing down the last touchpoint in the active client stage—the final touchpoint for a client while they are a client. This might be a celebration touchpoint or a final wrap-up work touchpoint. Or maybe it's a combination of both a celebration and final wrap-up touchpoint that provides a final work touchpoint and relationship touchpoint. Once you have the final active client stage touchpoint, start thinking about what you do after that. (If you are using the companion workbook, you can use the space provided to write down what you do now.)

How do you stay in touch or communicate with your clients post-work? Do you send a newsletter? Do you mail or email it? How often? Do you send a holiday card? Do you follow up with specific information at certain times of the year? If you need to, go back to the CX mapping activity in chapter 2 and see if you also deliver any of those touchpoints to your alumni clients. (Write those down in the associated section of the workbook, and put them in order, if applicable.)

The best way to determine how long someone will stay in your alumni client stage—and continue to receive touchpoints from you—is to consider what might be happening now. You might be doing nothing for alumni clients. But there's also a chance that you're delivering touchpoints without realizing it.

Sending holiday cards is the most common touchpoint I see with my clients. If you send a holiday card to your clients, and you never remove a client from the address list after they stop working with you, then, technically, you have an ongoing alumni client stage that continues indefinitely. If you only update the holiday card address list every three to five years, then your alumni client stage extends for those few years until your next update. But when the holiday cards stop is rarely an intentional choice. It's more likely haphazard: Often, the alumni client simply keeps receiving the holiday card until the business owner does a cleanup and decides to remove previous clients from the list.

You'll need to ask yourself how long it makes sense to have someone stay in your alumni client stage. As you move through this chapter, I'll ask you to consider some questions that will help you make that decision. Again, there is no right or wrong answer; you just need to decide. You can always change your mind later once the alumni client stage touchpoints are in execution mode.

Alumni Client Stage Best Practices

In the alumni client stage, you leave work touchpoints behind and concentrate solely on relationship touchpoints. Because the client is no longer active, there are no longer any work touchpoints for you to execute. In this stage, you have room to focus on sustaining a connection and the relationship.

Happily, the alumni client stage does not have to be complex or complicated. Just a few touchpoints throughout a year will help you stay connected to those who are the easiest to bring back as repeat clients or turn into referral sources. An old standby for doing this is the emailed newsletter, called the enewsletter, which works as a communication method and can be quite effective. In fact, most businesses send a monthly email newsletter to everyone on their list (clients, prospects, referral sources, contacts) with one message and call it a day.

But with these best practices, I encourage you to think outside of the enewsletter box because the truth is people will eventually stop paying attention to your newsletter message in their inbox. I'm not saying it's not helpful, but you need to elevate the other touchpoints you do for those in your alumni client stage. Here are a few best practices to consider.

Personalized Holiday Cards

I'm a big fan of sending personalized holiday cards to my clients, including alumni clients, and referral sources. For me, it's become a little bit of a competition with myself to try to outdo the previous years' cards, since we've been doing this for ten years. Our best card, hands down, was our 2020 Christmas card, where we showcased eleven different outfits and location changes for the Randall family to present the "12 Days of Covid." Even our dog, Evie, got into the action. I couldn't include the card in the book in a way that did it justice, but you can view the entire card on our reader-only resource page. But never fear, I do have another strong card contender to share—the one that started it all for our family, the 2015 Christmas card.

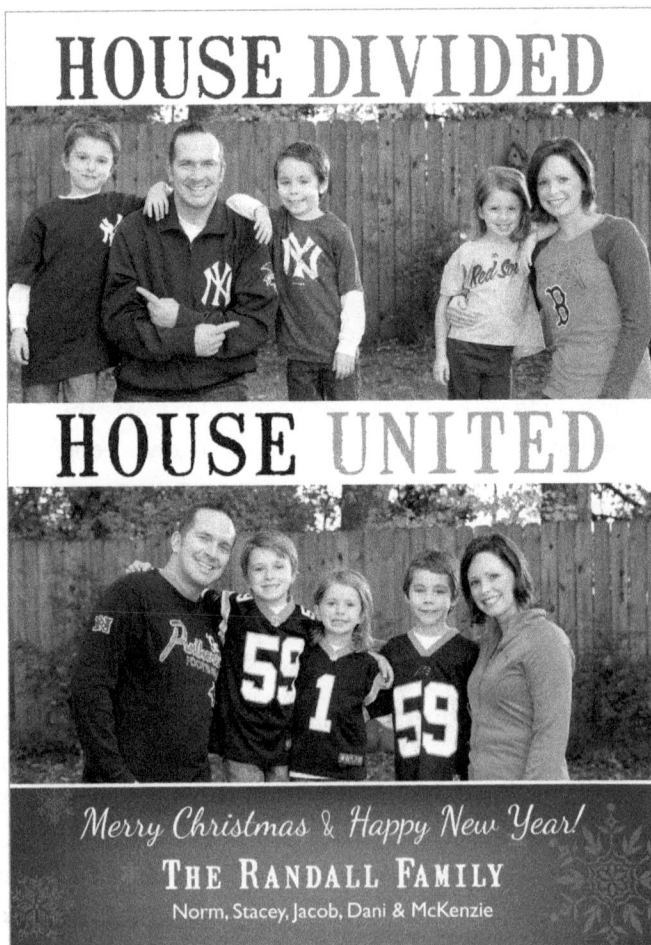

The 2015 Randall Family Christmas Card

We started sending personalized holiday cards in 2015 to share the news that we had become a family of five after we gained custody of our seven-year-old nephew. It seemed fitting to take our card to the next level with our "House Divided, House United" theme.

Our personalized holiday card has become a touchpoint staple for me with my client experience; clients in the new, active, and alumni client stages receive the card every year. This is an easy touchpoint to execute on for everyone and anchors the touchpoints for my alumni client stage.

I'm not advocating that you need to go to such depths with your personal or work holiday card; our family is an extreme case. I'm unfortunately competing against myself each year to come up with a unique and clever idea, and, while I love them, I'd be lying if I didn't admit they cause me a great deal of stress as well.

The idea of a personalized holiday card is to personalize it for you, however you define personal. It could feature your family, your team, employees, or the people you do life with, four-legged or otherwise. The point is to connect on a more intimate level than usual, so your alumni clients (plus everyone else who receives it) see you as the whole person you are, which is more than just your business.

Off-Guard Holidays

When I work with clients to create their alumni client stage, I look for easy, repeatable touchpoints. The holiday card I've outlined above is one of those because it comes around every year like clockwork, and can be sent to multiple groups of people. You can also do the same with off-guard holidays. Off-guard holidays are the less recognized holidays, like Mother's Day, Father's Day, and even Labor Day.

Recognizing off-guard holidays tends to be unexpected, which gives them more impact, more memorability. One option is to send a card. To stand out even more, you might consider sending a video that shares a personal message connected to the off-guard holiday. Keep it simple; it's the act of recognizing your alumni clients on this special holiday that has the power to connect.

Dates that Connect to Your Work

Finding an event or date that connects to the work you do can serve as a yearly touchpoint while also gently reminding your alumni clients you're still around. For this one, you're going to have to think through what touchpoint would have special significance because it's related to your business.

When I was a business and productivity coach, I would create fanfare around the National Day of Unplugging. It rolls around every year on the first Friday in March and goes from sunset on Friday through sunset on Saturday. While I promoted the day on social media for a more general audience, I always made sure that my alumni clients received the resources I sent out to help with unplugging for a day. Resources included a website for background, a downloadable tip sheet, and my encouragement that we could commit to a day of unplugging together. The point of this touchpoint was not to sell but to provide information and connect with my current and alumni clients with something related to the work I did.

Here are a few examples that you could consider depending on the work you do:

- If you own an IT company, you could promote National Computer Security Day on November 30 each year. One example would be to send out a tip sheet or checklist on how best to secure your laptop or passwords.

- If you're a financial professional, you could promote National Teach Children to Save Day, which rolls around each April. Send a bookmark with saving tips written for a child, or mail a small piggy bank with an encouraging note to ask their parents why saving is important.

Choosing the right touchpoints here can be rewarding, but please proceed with caution—if you want a touchpoint like this to have impact and be remembered, don't do it too often. Once a year is good, maybe twice if you have a really unique idea. But avoid the temptation to do it once a month, because at that frequency, your gesture will lose its value.

Considerations on Touchpoint Continuation

It is easiest to build the alumni client stage when you're thinking about that first year an alumni client is in that stage. But what happens when your clients hit the three-, five-, or ten-year mark? Over time, the sheer volume of clients moving into the alumni client stage each year can weigh the process down. To keep it simple, let me give you a few parameters in which to build the touchpoints for this stage.

We've been talking about maintaining relationships for a while, so it may come as a surprise that my next suggestion is this: Figure out when you will remove clients in the alumni client stage from a given touchpoint. To do this well, I suggest that you create parameters for each touchpoint in this stage, keeping in mind your industry standards. For example, in the real estate world, a known statistic is that people typically buy a house every seven years. For a real estate agent, it would make sense to craft an alumni client stage that keeps them connected to that alumni client for that range of time. For other business owners, keeping an alumni client in your alumni client stage for seven years would be considered a waste of resources if you receive no indication of the value of the connection. That's why you need to map out the touchpoints you want in your alumni client stage. You should also write down how long someone will receive the touchpoint before you stop sending it. (We have a sample of this built into the workbook if you're using it.)

Here are some of the boundaries my clients use when making this decision. Some reduce the number of touchpoints over time; for instance, they may plan for their first- and second-year alumni clients to receive a few more touchpoints than when they enter year three or four. Others extend the same number of touchpoints over the first few years, but when the client hits year five, they release them from the alumni client stage and the touchpoints altogether.

For those clients who decide to work with you again, they would drop back into your new client stage, and the client experience would start again. If at any point, a client—current or alumni—refers a client to you, you'll need to make sure you are also categorizing them as a referral source in addition to their client status.

Let's break down how this could potentially play out just with the best practices I mentioned above. In years one and two, the alumni clients would receive the most alumni touchpoints. For example, you could use the National Day of Unplugging (March) for a touchpoint that's connected to the work you do, an off-guard holiday like Mother's Day or Father's Day (May or June, respectively), an invite to your annual client appreciation event (September), and then your annual personalized holiday card (December) to round out the four touchpoints within your alumni client stage. For those clients who are not mothers or fathers, you could substitute with a touchpoint in the spring or at the start of summer. You would execute these four touchpoints in addition to your monthly or quarterly emailed newsletters if you send your newsletter to alumni clients.

When the alumni client moves into year three of the alumni client stage, however, and they haven't come back as a repeat client or started sending you referrals, then you need to decide if you're going to discontinue specific touchpoints for them. You might decide to let go of inviting them to your annual client appreciation event and the off-guard holiday touchpoint. Now, the only two touchpoints they would receive from you would be a touchpoint that connects to the work you do, such as the National Day of Unplugging from our example above, and your personalized holiday cards.

When the alumni client enters year five of the alumni client stage (and is still not a repeat client or referring you), you might remove them from this stage altogether. You would typically base a removal from the alumni client stage on budget, but also on what feels right for you and your business.

Getting Unstuck

We've covered a lot of ground in part 2, so I want to offer a reminder. If you're getting stuck on what it will take to execute on the new touchpoints you're bringing to your client experience, keep the following in mind: Your goal is to impact how your client *feels* while they are working with you. Go back to the Ideal Client Reaction script you completed in chapter 3 to help you decide which touchpoints will make them feel *good* about working with you. As you incorporate new touchpoints, remember why you're doing this work, even if it's as simple as staying front and center in their minds, and do it in a unique, caring, and resourceful way.

While you have been learning so much about how to improve your client experience, you may have lost sight of why you are doing it. But there's a good reason I started the book where I did: To receive referrals that you don't ask for, don't pay for, or feel like you have to take advantage of reciprocity to receive, you must first be referable. That only happens when you start with a referable client experience. At this point in the book, if you've done the exercises and then taken the extra step to start implementing what you built into your business, a referable client experience is well within your control.

Now let's bridge the gap from your referable client experience to generating referrals from your clients. How we do that is specific and unique.

Digital Downloads: Find the additional resources mentioned in this chapter on our reader-only resource page at referableclientexperience.com/ insider-resources.

PART 3

BRIDGE THE GAP TO REFERRALS

7

Understand the
Science of Referrals

ING.

It was that familiar text notification chime. Checking my phone, I noticed I had a text from a client, Liz, mentioning a friend and business owner she wanted to refer to me. But there was a catch. Her friend, we'll call her Julie, was a bookkeeper. Liz mentioned to Julie that she needed to talk to me to learn how I had helped her implement a successful referral strategy into her interior design business. Julie was interested but not sure she needed me. Julie shared with Liz that she had just started working with a business coach who was going to teach her how to market to her clients so they'd refer to her.

Ugh.

I had an immediate reaction of dread for Julie. Why? Because using general marketing tactics to generate referrals from clients is seldom productive. A marketing strategy will not produce referrals the way a referral strategy will. These are two very different strategies that use different tactics and require different language. Why is that?

Science. Specifically, the science of referrals. Let's break it down.

In the world of marketing, the type of tactics prescribed push the idea of referrals onto your clients. And that constant pushing—or reminding—violates the science of how referrals work. Referrals cannot be artificially created or manufactured. For referrals to work, they need to be your client's idea; clients refer someone to you because they know someone who needs you, someone who has a problem you can solve. Your client chooses to refer them to you because of this need. They are helping the person they know by referring them to you. That's what truly triggers referrals. The misguided idea behind marketing for referrals is that the constant reminding is what triggers referrals. It is not.

What you need to consider is that the marketing tactics might not match how you want to show up to your clients and show up in the marketplace. Worse, some tactics will make you feel terrible when you attempt them. Let's look at these awful techniques that so many pass off as referral-generating marketing tactics, and then I'll explain why these methods don't work.

What Won't Produce Referrals

I bet you've been told that you can receive referrals from your clients by marketing to them. Or by asking your clients to refer you, or by continually reminding your clients not to forget to refer. One marketing tactic you've heard you should do is to add a section to your monthly enewsletter that you email to clients with language about how you're open for referrals or saying that you'd appreciate referrals to people they know. Another tactic is to add a "referral page" to your website so clients can submit the name and contact information of a potential client they are referring to you. And I know you've seen this one—or maybe you've even created one yourself—a referral tagline for your email signature, like "Referrals are the greatest gift you can give me." I see this all the time, across all industries I work in. These tactics are built on the belief—common, though incorrect—that marketing to your clients will eventually bring them to a point where they will not only refer but refer a lot. But what they mostly succeed at is being gimmicky and overly promotional.

Other old-school, misguided marketing tactics spill over into meetings. You may have been told to find a few moments at the end of a client meeting to ask them to provide the names and contact information of people they know who would be a good fit for working with you. Or maybe you provide them with a list of those they are connected to on LinkedIn and ask them to connect you to them via email. Or maybe you have been told that you should send clients mass emails every two to three months, reminding them that they should be referring clients to you or that you are open to referrals.

I think the worst client referral tactic I have ever heard is the one where you tell your clients that there are two forms of payment required to work with you. In addition to the payment they will pay for your services, they will also "pay" you in referrals by having to refer a certain number of potential clients at the end of your time working together. I have even seen this secondary payment of referrals written into legal agreements that clients sign. I don't know about you, but the only form of payment a client owes me is money. Period.

I don't advise you to deploy any of those tactics to generate referrals. These gimmicky, poorly recommended methods only succeed in making you look desperate. I once stumbled across an article in *Entrepreneur* magazine with the title "25 Ways to Ask for a Referral Without Looking Desperate." You know it, and I know it: If you need twenty-five ways to not look desperate, it's because you know you feel desperate. This article aims to hype you up so you'll overlook how you feel—at your core—and ask for referrals anyway. The idea behind these twenty-five tactics is to push you past your (totally normal, by the way) feeling of desperation. The article preys on knowing that you feel desperate and awkward asking for referrals because feeling desperate sucks. Proceed with caution; the last thing you want is to *be seen as* desperate or needy. When that happens, your clients begin to doubt your expertise and your value to them.

These types of tactics *do* impact how your clients feel about you, but not in a good way. For example, if the client even notices the ask for referrals in your email signature (which they rarely do; clients typically focus on the message of your email, not your signature), the ask feels desperate and awkward. When you continually market to your clients to refer, ask them to refer, and remind them to refer, you quickly commoditize your relationship, and they tune out the request.

Even if you are willing to risk these negatives, this approach simply doesn't work. Instead, these tactics violate the science behind why and how referrals *do* work, which impacts your ability to successfully and sustainably generate referrals. This is why understanding the science behind referrals matters so much—you want to build and implement a referable client experience that is proven to produce referrals for you.

While marketing and asking tactics like those above have existed for what seems like generations, it doesn't make them right for you to deploy in your business. If you're still with me this far into the book, then you've innately felt that something was off with these gimmicky, marketing, or asking tactics as well. Let's look at a better way to do it.

Referrals Aren't About You

Here's what conventional tactics miss—and that no one talks about with referrals—your client, when connecting you to a new prospective client, wants it to be *their* idea. Not yours. When you tell them to refer someone to you (even if you frame it as a request), you create the feeling that you've just assigned them some work to do. And, to put it bluntly, they don't want to feel like they are doing your work for you.

When they initiate the referral, though, it doesn't feel like work. It feels like an opportunity to help someone they know by providing a resource that can help them solve their problem. You are just the resource, or the solution provider, within this storyline; you are not the hero. The hero is the one who is lending a helping hand to someone in need by referring them to you.

When your client offers to help solve someone's problem, the happiness trifecta of dopamine, serotonin, and oxytocin— the feel-good chemicals—fires in the brain. Not your brain, but your client's brain. Though it feels good for you to receive a referral, in this case, we're talking about how good it feels for your client to help someone they know. And, when your client refers to you for the first time, they also now become a new referral source for you.

This is what I mean when I say, "Referrals aren't about you." When you understand this fundamental part of the brain science and how the happiness trifecta in your client's (now referral source's) brain impacts the referral process, you can understand where you fit into the cast of referral characters. I know it might be tough to hear that you're not the star of this show or that the prospect isn't the star of the show either. You play, however, a vital role; consider yourself the third most important character out of three characters in the referral process. Your client is the hero, the prospect being referred to you is secondary, and you are the solution provider. It's important to know your place when clients are providing you with referrals. In your role, you're the one who helps the client do the thing they feel good about, which is helping someone they know by referring them to you for help.

What does this all mean? How you deploy referral-generation tactics within your client experience must respect the science of referrals and honor the relationship you have with your clients. Remember, your clients don't owe you referrals just because you did a great job. While you might deserve referrals for the work you do, you are not owed them.

Okay, now that you understand you aren't owed referrals and that you cannot violate the brain science of how referrals happen, it's time to dive into learning what you can do that will honor your relationships with your clients, deepen the connection you have with them, and have them start referring to you. Referrals from clients can happen in any client stage— new, active, or alumni—which is why you spent so much time on building your referable client experience in the first two parts of this book. If you're not referable, you can't just jump ahead, apply some referral seed language, and think everything is going to work out. In some cases, you'll learn how to

While you might deserve referrals for the work you do, you are not owed them.

plant referral seed language for specific moments, what I call "referral moments."

In other cases, you'll learn to plant referral seeds with work or relationship touchpoints because they happen within specific hot zones. And, finally, you'll learn how to plant referral seeds with the right people after you've identified them. We'll break all this down and tie it together with learning the right language to use in the next two chapters. The language piece is actually the easiest to implement within your client experience, as long as you have already built a referable client experience. So, let's knock out this final part.

Digital Downloads: Find the additional resources mentioned in this chapter on our reader-only resource page at referableclientexperience.com/insider-resources.

8

Identify Your Referral Hot Zones

A N APPLICATION RECEIVED notification popped into my inbox—a business owner, Lori, had applied to join my referral coaching program.

In the application form, Lori listed another client, Jen, as how she had heard about me. Jen was a brand new client. She had literally signed up for the program two days prior. Jen and I hadn't even had her onboarding call, as she was just starting on the prework that all of my clients complete before we dive into working together.

A few days later, during Jen's onboarding call, I brought up Lori. Jen wanted to know if Lori had applied and signed up, which made me laugh because this had unfolded so fast that Jen hadn't even received her thank-you note in the mail for referring Lori to me. During our conversation, Jen mentioned that after we had talked about her joining the coaching program, she'd instantly thought of Lori and knew she needed to join as well, so she had referred her.

I call clients like Jen the "right people." They're the ones who refer you really early in your client experience, almost before they've hired you. Typically, they also continue to refer, like Jen has.

I label them the "right people" because of one special quality that allows them to connect others with you so enthusiastically and so early. They are the type of people who think about making connections, sharing what they are doing, and looking for opportunities to see how they can help people. Many of us think and feel this way, but the right people are just more open to it, and they take quicker and more frequent action than the rest of us. It's almost like it's in their DNA. It is definitely in Jen's, and I benefited from that.

With the right people, the minute they decide to hire someone to work with or invest in something, they instantly think of others to tell and have reasons to share. Having the right people decide to work with you is amazing, but hard to duplicate because the right people are impossible to identify until the referral happens.

When it does happen, I encourage you to make the most of it by sending a handwritten thank-you card and making sure you have an outreach plan to take care of your referral sources (the people who refer to you). But it would be foolish to leave your future client referrals up to only the right people. While the right people are awesome, there are two more strategies I want you to put in place and leverage for the opportunity to plant referral seeds you can harvest later. One strategy identifies your business's hot zones, and the other tackles referral moments.

In this chapter, I'll break down what hot zones are and show you how to identify them in your business, as well as highlight some referral seeds you can plant within them. In the next chapter, I'll break down the language in even more detail and explain how to plant referral seeds in referral moments.

Decoding Referral Hot Zones

A hot zone is one of those points in time within your client experience when you have a greater likelihood you will receive referrals, not as a one-off but with some consistency. We refer to it as hot since you are more likely to receive referrals from clients when the client enters that moment or zone in your client experience. Knowing your hot zones helps you because you can leverage those points in time by adding the right referral language and touchpoint. To do that, you first need to identify if you have hot zones and when they happen.

The easiest way to do this is to reverse engineer when clients have referred you in the past. Limit your data gathering to client referrals only, not referrals from other sources, like centers of influence or contacts.

Unpacking Your Patterns

To really zero in on when you've received referrals in the past, you'll need to go back and find the data. I know data collection isn't fun or sexy, but it is a necessary and important step in the process. It doesn't have to be painful, I promise. I teach three different approaches to my clients, so you'll likely find a method that works well for you. Your options are the starter step, the master step, and the as-you-go step. Let me break down all three, and you decide which one fits best.

First, let's jump-start your thinking. Look over the following situations and determine if these are moments when you received referrals from clients:

- After a client signed up and got started
- At a certain point in the process
- When the client received specific results or a breakthrough
- When the client gave a testimonial
- When the client provided amazing feedback
- Six months or a year after they stopped working with you.

Regardless of which of the three steps you decide to use to complete this activity, just make sure you commit to completing one step in its entirety. (If you are using the companion workbook, just select one to complete and leave the other two blank.)

Starter Step

As with most things I teach, I recognize some folks just need to take a small step to get started. A step that seems too cumbersome or detailed is the fastest way for people to become demotivated so they don't do the work. If a small step—one that will start to paint a picture for you—is just what you need, then the starter step is the way to go. Here is the step-by-step process to get started; remember, it only works if you write it down.

1 Make a list of the past ten clients who were referred to you. You might be selecting ten clients from the past month, past quarter, or over the past year. This is not a list of the past ten clients who hired you, just the past ten clients who were referred to you.

2 Capture the names of the people who referred the clients to you. The person who referred a new client is called the referral source.

3 Look at your list of referral sources and mark the ones who are also your clients. This is important: Don't confuse this step and what you are working to uncover. Let me say it again: You need to differentiate which of the referral sources are clients. Give their names a star or circle them. If doing this digitally, maybe bold their name or highlight it in a different color. At this point, you'll have a list of clients who have also referred another client.

4 Next, you'll note *when* you received each referral and *where* in the client experience the referral source (referring client) was. Was the referral source just exiting your new client stage and moving into the active client stage when they referred you? Did they refer you after they stopped working with you and had moved into the alumni client stage? When you start noticing the "when," you'll begin to see what patterns emerge.

I'm not asking you to do an exhaustive analysis of every client with this method. From just a handful of clients, you will gain insight into when referrals might be happening, which provides you with some basic data about your referral hot zones. For some readers, this starter step is just enough to get them to take action. But others may want a complete picture of their hot zones. If that's you, you need to skip the starter step and move directly to the master step.

Master Step

The master step is the same as the starter step, with two important improvements. In this step, you will make a list of your referred clients and prospects over the past two years versus just the past ten referred clients. This gives you more opportunities to assess patterns. You'll follow a similar identification process with a few key changes. Here is the step-by-step process, and, again, it only works if you write it down.

1 Make a list of your clients from the past two years.

2 Make a list of your prospects from the past two years (those who did not or have not yet said yes to hiring you).

3 Remove anyone from both lists who was not referred to you, such as a client who came through advertising or the prospect you met at a networking meeting. You are only keeping clients and prospects who were referred to you on the list. To be referred, they had to have been referred by a human.

4 Capture the names of the people who referred the clients and prospects to you. The person who referred the client or prospect is called the referral source.

5 Look at your list of referral sources and mark the referral sources who are also your clients. These referring clients may have referred a client or a prospect. Give their names a star or circle it. If doing this digitally, maybe bold their name or highlight it in a different color.

6 Remove anyone from the list who referred a client or prospect to you who is not also a client. You only want clients on the list who also referred someone.

7 Note *when* you received each referral and *where* in the client experience the referral source (referring client) was. Was the referral source just exiting your new client stage and moving into the active client stage when they referred you? Did they refer you after they stopped working with you and

had moved into the alumni client stage? When you start noticing the *when*, you'll begin to see patterns emerge.

Because you are assessing a more robust set of data, two years plus clients and prospects referred to you, you'll be able to see if patterns emerge more quickly and which patterns are more prevalent in terms of when you receive referrals.

As-You-Go Step

If you've recently started your business or the starter and master steps feel like too much work, I have one more option for you. You can start tracking your potential hot zones today. Just keep one list where you track who clients referred and where your client is in their client stage with you when they referred. Next, make a note of what happened just before they referred. The more detailed you can get within the stage or what happened just prior to referring you, the better. This detail makes your pattern identification more reliable.

If you had asked me which hot zone produces the most referrals for my business, without going through the master step, I would have told you about 10 percent of my referrals come in the new client stage. Turns out, I was wrong. This stage represents more than 25 percent of my referrals. Knowing this allows me to make specific adjustments to my new client stage.

Common Hot Zones

Pattern identification data will always be the best route to determining your hot zones. But allow me to offer you a shortcut. In my work with clients, I find there are usually four main hot zones. They are:

1   Right after a new client starts working with you (new client
    stage),

2   After early results are received (new or active client stage),

3   Work delivered or results received (active client stage),

4   Finished working with you (alumni client stage).

Let me walk you through a few examples. If you receive referrals from clients right after you start working with them, that
is a hot zone in the new client stage, and the anticipation of
the awesomeness to come is what drives these clients to refer.
For example, if you mapped out how you're going to get results
with your client—maybe using the Expectation Map you built
in chapter 4—their anticipation of seeing how it feels to work
with you can drive referrals if they have an opportunity to refer.

As another example, if you receive referrals after the work
you do provides early results for your clients, then that is a
referral hot zone in the active client stage. To explain how this
works in my business, there is one tactic I teach my clients to
jump-start referrals. Sometimes it leads to multiple referrals in
a short time frame. The surprise factor of how well that single
tactic works drives them to talk about their success and then
to refer because they are blown away. Again, while the results
drive them to want or be willing to refer, the opportunity still
has to exist by there being someone to refer.

If you receive referrals after you complete the client
engagement, that is typically at the end of the active client
stage, just before they move into the alumni client stage.
For example, your main work deliverable might be the fully
funded estate plan, a newly created brand look and launched
website, finally having their business accounting cleaned up
and organized within the bookkeeping software, or a newly

You should focus on those moments within your client experience that have a greater chance to direct the thinking of your clients to refer you.

renovated and styled home. The completion of the work, coupled with their excitement (or relief) over what they now have, drives their willingness to refer.

If you receive referrals after a client has finished working with you—could be a few weeks, months, or years later—this is the alumni client stage. That they are still connected to you with positive feelings beyond simply working with you is what drives the referrals.

Why Hot Zones Matter

So why does all this matter? Because there's more than just luck involved. You might not have thought so—there is a very good possibility you believe that when referrals show up, it's by chance. Sometimes it is. But when the person who might refer you has a clear *opportunity* to refer you, that's when referrals happen. That's why you should focus on those moments within your client experience that have a greater chance to direct the thinking of your clients to refer you.

If you do this, will all clients refer you? No, even if they love working with you and have provided you with the best testimonials. Some just won't refer, no matter what you do. I tell my clients to aim for a baseline of 20 to 30 percent of their clients referring to them and then grow from there to increase the percentage of clients referring to you.

Identifying your hot zones is the best place to start. Once you have identified your hot zones, you can decide to add a relationship-based touchpoint to the hot zone and layer in referral seed language as well. But first, you need to map out your specific hot zones.

Mapping Out Your Hot Zones

Using the data you gathered from either the starter, master, or as-you-go steps, map out your hot zones. Then align those hot zones to the client stages. (You can map this out from a timeline perspective in the companion workbook.) So that you can see how this works, I'll take two of the common hot zones I provided earlier and show you how to connect them to the client stage, plus how to extend the opportunity to add in a relationship-building touchpoint.

Leveraging Common Hot Zones

When I'm working with a client, my goal within an identified hot zone for referrals is to add a relationship touchpoint so we can deepen the relationship with the client and plant a referral seed to direct how the client thinks about the business owner and referring to them. Sometimes we can do both with the same touchpoint, and sometimes we can only do one. Let me show you both options so you can see them in action.

Touchpoint with No Language

If you uncovered that you do receive some referrals from clients after they recently started working with you (during the new client stage), then the best option is to focus on deepening the connection and strengthening the excitement they feel in working with you. A best practice example from chapter 4 could be to send a handwritten card or welcome gift. Because your objective with a new client stage welcome gift is to also overcome any pangs of buyer's remorse, the focus of the touchpoint would just be relationship-building; you're not focused on trying to also weave in and plant any referral seed language. This doesn't mean you can't plant a referral seed, but you must do it with delicacy since trust development is still in its growing phase. If you focus more on wowing your client by acknowledging how they are feeling, they will remember that for longer.

Touchpoint with Language

Now let's look at another example: when a client finishes working with you. This is when the active client stage is ending, and the client is moving into the alumni phase. One touchpoint you could do now is to give them a shout-out on social media—and tag them—to celebrate their business, the work they did with you, or the results they achieved while working with you. This is not a new idea, but you're going to take it a step further in two ways. First, if the client you are posting about was referred to you, then you can tag the person who referred them to you (the referral source) with a shout-out thanking them for the referral. In some cases, you may need to ask permission, and in certain industries, you may not be able to do this. If it's something you can do, then certainly do it. Second, wait a few days after the post appears on social media platforms and then follow up with your client about the post. More than likely, at this point, they have probably liked the post, commented on it, and possibly even shared it with their online network. When you reach out, ask what they thought about the post: Did they receive comments, feedback, or questions from others?

Keep your language light; this is a conversation. Above all, please resist the urge to say something like, "Well, if anyone mentioned the post to you, then you should refer them to me right away by connecting us via email." Don't say that. That's *asking*, and it's making the referral your idea, which is the fastest way to shut someone down from referring you.

Instead, shift your language to plant a referral seed, like this, "If you get questions specific to the work we did together, I can answer them so you don't have to. Just connect us however is easiest, through direct message or email, and I'll be happy to answer their questions."

I know for some people that subtle shift in language will feel like you are beating around the bush rather than coming out directly and saying what you really want to happen. But remember, generating referrals isn't about you. How you go about generating referrals must protect the relationship with your client, create the environment where it comes up as their idea, and respect the science of referrals. This subtle shift in language allows the idea of referrals to percolate in the minds of your clients. Even if from that one touchpoint—in this case, the social media post—they do not refer you right away, you must trust the process that you have planted a referral seed. Now it's your job to continue to water and nurture those referral seeds, so let's dig deeper into understanding the power of the right referral seed language.

Digital Downloads: Find the additional resources mentioned in this chapter on our reader-only resource page at referableclientexperience.com/insider-resources.

9

The Secret Is in the Language

H E THOUGHT HE WOULD be fine doing it his way.

Never mind that Bob (not his real name), an independent financial advisor, had hired me to help him generate more referrals. While he was on the right path regarding the type of touchpoints he did for clients, he balked at the tiny language tweak I had asked him to make.

"I don't think it'll really matter," he said on a call. "My clients love working with me and appreciate the work we do. I don't think I need to add in the referral seeds. It seems so minor and nuanced. I'll just keep what I am doing and add in some of your touchpoint suggestions."

He thought he knew better.

He was wrong.

Months later, he shared that he hadn't received any referrals.

I responded, "I'm not surprised. You haven't been planting referral seeds within any of your touchpoints, so you aren't subtly directing how your clients think about you. Planting referral seeds may seem minor because it is easy and simple to do, but it is powerful. Without it, you have a referable client experience that's not generating any referrals."

I don't want you to follow in Bob's shoes. Think of the time wasted and referrals missed. You have come so far in building out your referable client experience, and you're now working to connect it to receiving referrals from your clients. But you will need to add one last ingredient to add fuel to the fire, and that is the language you use. As you've probably figured out, referral seeds are the words you use to "plant" the idea of referrals without ever having to ask for referrals, offer to pay for them, or use referrals in your marketing in a gimmicky or promotional way. I once explained referral seeds this way: If the touchpoints you deliver on are considered the meat and potatoes, then the language you use is the special sauce you add that makes the dinner taste amazing. By language, I mean referral seeds. You plant referral seeds to encourage the idea of referrals to germinate in the mind of your clients.

Let's unpack using referral seeds by starting with what not to do first and then looking at referral moments you need to be able to recognize.

What Not to Do with Referral Seeds

I can predict three ways you might fail to use referral seeds correctly. The first is to be like my client Bob who decided not to use the right language at all—and choose not to plant referral seeds.

Another way people doom their efforts is by not approaching the language they are going to use with a level of discernment and not taking the time to get comfortable with the language for a particular touchpoint or referral moment. You can only gain confidence by practicing, using this language, and then assessing how it goes for you. Your comfort and confidence are important because referral seeds work when they come across as genuine and when they sound like the way you talk—they must fit you.

Finally, the third way that you could fail to use referral seeds correctly is to oversaturate by planting them everywhere, for everyone, all the time. There is an optimal cadence, a rhythm to planting referral seeds so they work. I can't give you an exact number of times to plant referral seeds with each client, but if you keep your language natural, plant the referral seed when it makes sense and has been shown to work (from your hot zone mapping), you will germinate the idea of clients referring to you as they move through your client experience. You need to be intentional in the language you use to plant referral seeds with your clients.

Now that you know what not to do when using and planting referral seeds, let's look at moments in your client experience where you can plant referral seeds. But please—allow me to say this again—even though you won't know every referral seed you can plant during the client experience from just reading this book, you do have enough examples to overuse the referral seeds. So don't. Practice discernment, not oversaturation.

Let's look at a few referral moments where you can plant a referral seed. Pay attention to whether any of these overlap with your hot zones.

When a Client Is Referred

One easy referral seed you can plant throughout the client experience is an occasional reminder about being referred to the client who was referred to you themselves. From time to time, you could say something like this: "I'm so glad [insert name of person who referred] referred you to me so we have the opportunity to work together."

This one is simple and doesn't need much explanation. As a reminder, you can only use this if the client themselves was referred to you. While you can plant this seed a couple of times during their work with you, don't overdo it.

Future Pacing Referrals

There are a couple of referral seeds I teach my clients to plant where the goal is to future pace referrals. One future pacing scenario: When you invite clients to a client appreciation event, even if they are alumni clients, use language in the invitation that goes beyond thanking them for their support. Instead of the typical language, such as, "We'd like to invite you to our client appreciation event as a thanks for being a client and for your continued support," go one step further and modify the line to say, "We appreciate your support of our firm in being a client, referring clients to us, and advocating for us." While not every client receiving the client appreciation invite would have referred to you, it does position that referrals are received from clients, but in a subtle way that is a natural part of the event.

Referral Seed After a Client Refers

I know I touched on this language piece in my first book, *Generating Business Referrals Without Asking*, but it is critical, so I would be remiss if I didn't include it here. When a client *does* refer you, please do three things:

1 Handwrite a thank-you card and mail it to them (not an email or text). You can email or text to quickly say thank you right after the referral comes in—but also write the handwritten thank-you note. Here's the language to use in the thank-you card:

"I just want to say thank you for referring [insert prospect's name] to me. It is a pleasure to help those you know and care about."

Always remember to ask yourself, why should a client refer you again if you can't thank them for the referral they just sent you?

2 Track who they referred, the date they referred, and at what point in the client experience journey the client is in when they referred you.

3 Make a note of who they referred in their client file and remind yourself, and/or your team members, to verbally thank them a few times over the next few work touchpoints.

And because it bears repeating: Please don't overdo it with planting referral seeds. More referral seeds planted will not produce more referrals or produce referrals faster. In fact, your extra efforts will have the opposite effect. While there is no point in the client experience when you are guaranteed referrals, there are moments throughout the client experience where you can build more loyalty and impact how your clients feel with relationship touchpoints by leveraging hot zones and referral moments and planting referral seeds. Focus first on becoming referable and then on receiving referrals from your client experience.

Focus first on becoming
referable and then
on receiving referrals from
your client experience.

The Real Lifetime Value of Referrals

I probably don't have to explain the value of receiving referrals to you, especially if you've made it to the end of this book. You know how powerful referrals can be to your growth, especially when you receive referrals consistently. This makes your clients more valuable than ever. Typically, the real lifetime value of a client is viewed as the money they initially spent when they first signed up, or in their first year, plus any upsells or repeat business they will give you. But expand your vision to 360 degrees, and you'll see that lifetime value also includes the increase in value that occurs when the client is referring you. The 360-degree view takes into account the money they initially spend in year one, plus any upsells or repeat business, plus the referrals they give you. If you do it right, the referrals they give you should continue year after year.

Digital Downloads: Find the additional resources mentioned in this chapter on our reader-only resource page at referableclientexperience.com/ insider-resources.

Conclusion

"**I**S THIS HOW IT WORKS?" Kathleen asked, lowering her voice as she leaned forward in her chair, as if she didn't want anyone else in the coffee shop to hear what she was about to ask.

"What do you mean?" I asked.

"In the first week of working with you—really before I've started doing anything—I've had two clients refer me." She smiled broadly. "It feels a little bit like magic."

I laughed. "It is definitely not magic. Have you heard the saying that what you focus on grows? It comes from understanding how the reticular activating system works in our brain."

"Oh, like seeing red cars—that study that was done years ago?"

"Yes, exactly."

The general explanation of the Red Car Theory is that when you want something or focus on it, you see more of it. If you want to buy a red car, you suddenly start seeing red cars everywhere. Since Kathleen had decided to invest in growing referrals in her consulting business, she was starting to see them more clearly.

This isn't the first time I've seen this happen with my clients receiving early referrals after saying yes to working with me. Eryn Morgan, the business coach for creative entrepreneurs I introduced in chapter 3, shared that in the first week of joining my coaching program, she received a huge referral. She was absolutely correct when she shared, "I believe it happening so quickly was a result of saying yes to myself and to working with you. I had a quick win like this come in when I needed it most."

What you focus on and make a commitment to will start to grow. As you map out your client experience, add better relationship touchpoints, leverage your referral hot zones, and plant the right referral seed language, you will start to notice referrals differently in your business. While results may not be as quick as they were for Kathleen and Eryn, if you commit to putting into action what you have learned in this book and start tracking your results, you will be able to watch them build over time.

Once your elevated, referable client experience is in place, it'll be time for you to start tracking your results. Please make sure you are tracking every referral you receive and when you received it, so you can see if your strategy is working. Referrals may grow slowly so you should actually anticipate that. But stay committed to the ongoing process so each client receives your repeatable and referable client experience.

When you do start seeing success and start getting the feedback you wanted when you created your Ideal Client Reaction script, please make sure to share with me via email or on social media so I can cheer on your success.

What you focus on and make a commitment to will start to grow.

Referable Client Experience First, Then Referrals

I'm about to sound like a broken record, but please indulge me for this final page or two of the book. Remember, you first need to make sure you have a client experience in place that makes you referable. No tactic or language tip I give you will overcome a poor or choppy client experience. Of course, if you mapped out your current client experience in chapter 2 and then used the best practices to level up the experience in the new client stage (chapter 4), active client stage (chapter 5), and alumni client stage (chapter 6), you should be well on your way to building a referable client experience. And as you have learned, the goal of your client experience is to evoke the right emotions from your clients.

That's because evoking the right emotions from your clients deepens your relationship with them. And how your clients feel about you is directly tied to how they think about you—and if they will talk about you to others, specifically to refer you. If you can impact how your clients feel—genuinely and authentically—you can then direct how they think about you. You use the right moments plus the right language to be able to plant the idea of referrals with your clients.

When you do it right, you gain a little wow factor. Your efforts will lead your clients to say: "I just didn't expect that from working with you."

That surprise is the wow factor they'll remember you for.

Digital Downloads: Find the additional resources mentioned in this chapter on our reader-only resource page at referableclientexperience.com/insider-resources.

Acknowledgments

T o NORM, my husband, who always believes in me and what I'm capable of, thank you for your constant support and on-demand grilled cheeses.

To my kids—McKenzie, Jacob, and Danny—you can do anything you're willing to work toward. But work is ... well ... work, so make sure it's something you enjoy.

To my mom, Mary Ella, and my dad, Steve, in heaven—thank you for being the kind of parents willing to raise a confident woman.

To my business bestie and bestie in life, Amy Collins. While your constant "Is it done yet?" refrain grew quite tiresome, I appreciate that you never let me settle for less than what I am capable of.

To my clients and alumni clients, seeing you do the work and put the referral strategies in place—while reaping the rewards of increased referrals—is a constant reminder that together we make it happen. Each of you makes my business the massive blessing it is.

To AJ Harper, author of *Write a Must-Read*. Thank you for taking the time to learn about this second book of mine and thinking enough of it and me to refer me to Jesse Finkelstein at Page Two.

To my publishing and editing team at Page Two, including Jesse Finkelstein, Natassja Barry, Marni Seneker, Sheila Trask, Merlina McGovern, Rachel Ironstone, Madelaine Manson, Viktoria Skaper, Jennifer Lum, and the rest of the team, thank you for helping me bring this book to life and, in the process, helping me become a stronger writer (though sometimes I did it kicking and screaming).

Notes

Chapter 1: What Is It Like to Work with You?

13   *This meant the client experience was*: Dave Fish and Brian Keehner, "A Brief History of Customer Experience," CustomerThink, August 24, 2018, customerthink.com/a-brief-history-of-customer-experience/.

14   *According to Customer Experience Matters, a business advisory firm*: Bruce Temkin, "Customer Experience Leads to Recommendations (Charts for 20 Industries)," Customer Experience Matters, February 23, 2017, experiencematters.wordpress.com/category /roi-of-customer-experience/; Bruce Temkin, "Report: ROI of Customer Experience, 2014," Customer Experience Matters, September 9, 2014, experiencematters.wordpress. com/2014/09/09/report-roi-of-customer-experience-2014/.

14   *A 2025 Forrester study of customer experience leaders revealed that*: Riccardo Pasto and Katy Cobian, "Budget Planning Guide 2025: Customer Experience," Forrester, August 1, 2024, reprint.forrester .com/reports/budget-planning-guide-2025-customer-experience- 54f3ee10/index.html.

15   *For example, back in 2020, a Gartner survey revealed that*: "Gartner Says 74% of Customer Experience Leaders Expect Budgets to Rise in 2020," press release, Gartner, January 15, 2020, gartner.com /en/newsroom/press-releases/2020-01-15-gartner-says-74--of-- customer-experience-leaders-expe.

15   *Going even further back to 2014, a Gartner survey forecasted that*: Jake Sorofman, "Agenda Overview for Customer Experience, 2015," Gartner, December 22, 2014, gartner.com/imagesrv/digital -marketing/pdfs/agenda-overview-for-customer.pdf.

16   *For example, Forrester defines client experience as*: Harley Manning,
      "Customer Experience Defined," blog post, Forrester, November 23,
      2010, forrester.com/blogs/definition-of-customer-experience/.

16   *Others, like HubSpot, define client experience as*: Rami El-Abidin,
      "Customer Experience: What It Is and Why It's Important [+Data-
      Backed Tips]," blog, HubSpot, updated June 11, 2024, blog.hubspot
      .com/service/what-is-customer-experience.

19   *In other words, they believe that their ability to stand out against
      their competition*: "New Research from Dimension Data Reveals
      Uncomfortable CX Truths," press release, Dimension Data,
      April 4, 2017, prnewswire.com/news-releases/new-research
      -from-dimension-data-reveals-uncomfortable-cx-truths
      -300433878.html.

Chapter 4: Nail the New Client Stage

56   *Businesses can lose anywhere from 20 to 80 percent of new clients*:
      "Never Lose Another Customer (With Joey Coleman, Founder
      and 'Chief Experience Composer' of Design Symphony)," Success
      Network, thesuccessnetwork.tv/never-lose-another-customer-with
      -joey-coleman-founder-and-chief-experience-composer-of-design
      -symphony/.

Chapter 5: Master the Active Client Stage

76   *A study by Bain & Company found that increasing client retention
      rates*: "Retaining customers is the real challenge," Bain & Company,
      January 2006, bain.com/insights/retaining-customers-is-the
      -real-challenge/.

Chapter 6: Extend the Alumni Client Stage

89   *But humans have the attention span of a goldfish*: Jill Ebstein,
      "Our Attention Span Is Shorter Than a Goldfish's. Here's What
      We Can Do About It," *Orlando Sentinel*, updated July 6, 2021,
      orlandosentinel.com/2021/07/06/our-attention-span-is-shorter
      -than-a-goldfishs-heres-what-we-can-do-about-it-commentary/.

Chapter 7: Understand the Science of Referrals

106 *I once stumbled across an article in* Entrepreneur *magazine*:
John Rampton, "25 Ways to Ask for a Referral Without Looking
Desperate," *Entrepreneur*, April 11, 2017, entrepreneur.com
/growing-a-business/25-ways-to-ask-for-a-referral-without
-looking-desperate/292645.

107 *When your client offers to help solve someone's problem*: Eva Ritvo,
"The Neuroscience of Giving," *Psychology Today*, April 24, 2014,
psychologytoday.com/us/blog/vitality/201404/the-neuroscience
-giving.

Conclusion

133 *The general explanation of the Red Car Theory*: "The Red Car Theory:
Why You See What You Focus On," Disabled Entrepreneur UK,
February 15, 2025, msn.com/en-gb/health/mindandbody/the-red
-car-theory-why-you-see-what-you-focus-on/ar-AA1pw4bq.

About the Author

Carrie Allen of Carrie Allen, LLC

STACEY BROWN RANDALL is on a mission to keep business owners from business failure. Through her one-on-one and group programs, she teaches business owners how to generate referrals naturally—without manipulating, incentivizing, or even asking.

Brown Randall is a national speaker and the host of the *Roadmap to Referrals* podcast. She has been featured in national publications like *Entrepreneur* magazine, *Investor's Business Daily*, *Forbes*, and more. She is the multiple award-winning author of *Generating Business Referrals Without Asking* and coauthor with LuAnn Nigara of *A Well-Designed Business—The Power Talk Friday Experts*.

Brown Randall is married with three kids and lives with her family in North Carolina.

staceybrownrandall.com.

Learn More

HAVE A GROUP OR BOOK CLUB READING THE BOOK?
Stacey would love to virtually join one of your book club
meetings for an author Q&A where your group can ask her
questions about the book. Just submit your information at
staceybrownrandall.com/speaking.

You can also learn more about working with Stacey Brown
Randall at staceybrownrandall.com. She works with clients in
a variety of ways—online, in groups, and in person—so you can
work with her in the way you learn and implement best.

www.ingramcontent.com/pod-product-compliance
Lightning Source LLC
Chambersburg PA
CBHW030522210326
41597CB00013B/995